THE
DEMOCRACY
AMENDMENTS

THE
DEMOCRACY
AMENDMENTS

How to Amend Our
U.S. Constitution
to Rescue Democracy
for All Citizens

Rick Hubbard

Concerned Citizens Press
South Burlington, Vermont

The Democracy Amendments
Rick Hubbard

Copyright © 2016 by Rick Hubbard

Concerned Citizens Press
South Burlington, Vermont

www.concernedcitizenspress.com

To purchase in bulk, contact the publisher
rick@concernedcitizenspress.com

ISBN 978-0-9983316-0-7

Contents

Preface

Our democracy is in trouble and we the people know it. Our U.S. political system is completely distorted as it's currently financed and structured. Problems with the way we select our political leaders have been on full display in the 2016 Presidential election.

Once elected, Washington politicians are not equally and properly representing our broad citizen interests, since they regularly tip outcomes of law, policy, and regulation toward the interests of wealthy and influential campaign donors.

These actions regularly move large amounts of money out of our pockets and into theirs, distort and often delay action on matters important to our welfare, and undermine the very purpose of citizen representation our founding fathers worked to provide for us in our Constitution. This adversely affects the vast majority of us, regardless of whether we are conservative, moderate, liberal, or of some other ideology.

Amending our Constitution to achieve needed reforms is the paramount public policy issue of our time. Congress has refused to effectively act for decades. Thus it's up to us — we the people — to initiate constitutional amendments to repair it.

But first we must decide how to best accomplish reform. Will we really fix the problem, or as most current amendment proposals would do, just fix a part, in a way that would not resolve the underlying real problem?

This book sets a high bar for discussion of all amendment proposals. In it, I propose the wording and reasoning for a comprehensive 28th Amendment to result in complete reform of the way we structure and finance our political system.

If we citizens are going to get excited about reforming our democracy, let's be bold and build a movement to fully and comprehensively amend our U.S. Constitution to regain full citizen control of our democracy. Together, we can accomplish this. Let's do it!

Dedication

Granny "D"
Doris Haddock

Original photo credit John Parker

This book is dedicated to a woman who's particularly special to me. She symbolizes all the citizens in America who understand the importance of restoring our democracy, and with it the equality of citizen participation in our political system.

Specifically, I speak of committed, persevering Doris Haddock of Dublin New Hampshire, known affectionately to many of us simply as "Granny D," who died on March 9th, 2010 at age 100.

I first heard of Granny D on Christmas Day of 1998 due to an odd coincidence. My life-partner Sally and I had driven to Redding, CT for an annual holiday gathering of her extended family. Twenty or so of us were gathered in the living room at Aunt Rosy's house for drinks to be followed by Christmas dinner. I was talking to Joe, a young man recently married to Sally's niece, when for some reason he began to tell me about his grandmother who had this crazy idea of walking across the entire United States to highlight the need to reform our democracy, and the family couldn't talk her out of it.

As I recall our conversation, the family had tried everything they could think of to discourage her. "How will you accomplish this?," they asked. "I'll walk 10 miles a day, 6 days a week," she answered. "How do you know you can walk 10 miles a day, 6 days a week? Prove it," they said. So out she went, walking 10 miles a day for 6 days. "Where will you stay at night?" they asked. "I'll sleep out overnight unless people I meet take me in," she said. "Prove that you can camp out overnight," they said. So off she went with her sleeping bag and overnight gear, hiking 10 miles, sleeping overnight, and then returning home. Granny D simply jumped over every hurdle her family placed in her way.

Not being able to discourage her, the family finally said okay, they'd support her!

One week later on New Year's Day, 1999, Granny D, then 88, began her walk across America from Pasadena, California to highlight the importance of reforming the way we finance our political process in order to strengthen our democracy and its representation of all citizens. Through her many television, newspaper and radio interviews and appearances, and also through her website, she reached hundreds of thousands of American citizens to raise awareness about how big campaign contributions from special interests adversely affect the vast majority of American citizens.

Ignoring her bad back, arthritis, and emphysema, she completed the 3,200-mile trip in 14 months, shortly after her 90th birthday, arriving in Washington on February 29, 2000, to the tune of 2,200 supporters chanting, "Go, Granny, Go!" She brought with her petition signatures from thousands of American citizens demanding that Congress enact meaningful reform.

Some two months later, Granny D and other supporters returned to Washington on April 21st where she and 31 others were arrested for demonstrating in the Capitol building. Subsequently, on Wednesday, May 24, 2000 she appeared in court in the District of Columbia to plead guilty to the charge.

Below, are pertinent parts of her remarks before the Judge.

"Your Honor, the old woman who stands before you was arrested for reading the Declaration of Independence in America's Capitol Building. I did not raise my voice to do so and I blocked no hall."

'The First Amendment to the Constitution, Your Honor, says that Congress shall make no law abridging the freedom of speech, or of the press; or the right of the people peaceably to assemble, and to petition the Government for a redress of grievances, so I cannot imagine what legitimate law I could have broken.'

'I was reading from the Declaration of Independence to make the point that we must declare our independence from the corrupting bonds of big money in our election campaigns.'

'And so I was reading these very words when my hands were pulled behind me and bound: "We hold these truths to be self-evident, that all men are created equal, that they are endowed by their Creator with certain

unalienable Rights, that among these are Life, Liberty and the pursuit of Happiness. — That to secure these rights, Governments are instituted among Men, deriving their just powers from the consent of the governed, — That whenever any form of Government becomes destructive of these ends, it is the Right of the People to alter or to abolish it.'

'Your Honor, we would never seek to abolish our dear United States. But alter it? Yes. It is our constant intention that it should be a government of, by and for the people, not the special interests....'

'Your Honor, to the business at hand: the old woman who stands before you was arrested for reading the Declaration of Independence in America's Capitol Building. I did not raise my voice to do so and I blocked no hall. But if it is a crime to read the Declaration of Independence in our great hall, then I am guilty."[1]

The judge, Chief Judge Hamilton of the DC federal district court, was silent after Doris made her statement. In sentencing, he said to Doris and the demonstrators:

"As you know, the strength of our great country lies in its Constitution and her laws and in her courts. But more fundamentally, the strength of our great country lies in the resolve of her citizens to stand up for what is right when the masses are silent. And, unfortunately, sometimes it becomes the lot of the few, sometimes like yourselves, to stand up for what's right when the masses are silent, because not always does the law move so fast and so judiciously as to always be right. But given the resolve of the citizens of this great country, in time, however slowly, the law will catch up eventually."[2]

Granny D inspired me, as she also did for so many others, to re-dedicate myself to do as much as possible to bring about comprehensive reform.

Unfortunately, despite the efforts of Doris and many others of us, Congress has not effectively acted in the intervening 16 years. In fact the systemic corruption of our political process is worse than ever, and most members of Congress have little incentive to fix it, since it serves their interests in remaining in power, just as it serves the interests of the tiny fraction of the wealthiest amongst us to continue to finance their campaigns to keep them in power. The rest of us continue to be adversely affected from this, regardless of whether we are conservative, moderate, liberal or pro-gressive.

So if Congress won't act, it's up to us — we the people — to act. The framers of our Constitution have provided us with a way.

Repairing the way we finance and structure our federal political system so our Washington politicians will again properly provide equality of representation of the interests of the vast majority of American citizens is, as phrased by the Honorable Phil Hoff, Vermont's former Governor, *"The paramount issue of our time, for it goes to the very core of our democracy and representation."*[3]

So I ask you: "If you're not already working on this, why not?"

Introduction

The case for why we citizens need to reform our democracy has already been repeatedly made, in many different ways, in recent decades. Therefore this book does not repeat what so many other writers have already covered.

These days, few even bother to argue that our political system properly works to equally serve our interests. Most of us already know we've got a problem. Some of us know it in our gut — as in: "The system is rigged. It doesn't represent me. It's making decisions that make life harder for me. It doesn't listen to me. Why bother to vote." Others know it as a corruption of our very system of government, of the ideals of equal representation that our founders worked hard to build into our Constitution, and these citizens are also upset and want it fixed. But if you'd like to read and absorb further detail about the problem itself, please refer to Appendix A at the end of this book where I've listed several good books on the subject, together with summaries of their contents.

Out of all of these books, I'd most recommend Harvard professor and activist Lawrence Lessig's 2016 edition of *Republic, Lost — The Corruption of Equality and the Steps to End It*.[4] It's perhaps the most recent, up-to-date, and comprehensive book on the subject. Professor Lessig makes the case for reform in great and convincing detail, and also presents his thoughts on how to improve the present system.

Unfortunately, despite enormous evidence, coupled with calls for reform over the past several decades, Congress has refused to act, by either enacting statutes or by amending our U.S. Constitution, to repair the way we govern ourselves to provide true equality of representation for the interests of all its citizens.

Little has been achieved, largely because it's not in the interest of Congress to repair a political system that currently provides politicians with immense advantages to get re-elected and remain in power. Similarly, both the Republican and Democratic parties have huge incentive to act in their own best interests to, when out of power, return to power. Since the shared interests of citizens often conflict with the interests of those wealthy funders of candidate's campaigns, politicians "lean to the green" to be sure to have the huge amounts of money needed to campaign for re-election. In return, they distort and tip laws, regulations, and policies toward the interests of their funders, rather than toward the broader interests of their constituents

Fortunately the framers of our Constitution anticipated that a corrupted Congress itself could be the problem.

On September 15, 1787 as the Convention was reviewing the Article V revisions relating to Amendment, as made by the Committee of Style, George Mason, delegate from Virginia, expressed opposition to the provisions limiting the power to propose amendments to Congress. According to the Convention records, Mason thought that "no amendments of the proper kind would ever be obtained by the people, if the Government should become oppressive, as he verily believed would be the case." Mason's argument was successful in convincing the framers that such a Congress would likely fail to act in order to prevent itself from being reformed.[5]

For this reason, our framers provided an alternate way we citizens can initiate an amendment process, by having our respective state legislatures call for a convention to propose amendments to repair our process of government. And no matter how many separate amendments arise from this convention, only those with sufficient support to become subsequently ratified by three fourths of the states — thirty-eight — can become valid amendments to the Constitution by which we govern ourselves.

Such is the situation we find ourselves in today. For the more than forty years I'm personally familiar with, Congress has been asked many times by various groups and individuals to enact comprehensive reforms. And despite occasional tiny bits of reform, there has never been any real systemic reform.

While it would be great if Congress would act, for it's certainly quicker and easier, this book is based upon the realistic assumption that, for the reasons previously mentioned, it's either unlikely to happen, or Congress will only initiate marginal improvements which are not significant enough to truly produce real reform.

Since Congress has refused to act, it's time for we the people to act if we want truly comprehensive reform. Together we must carefully discuss, fully debate, and ultimately build consensus on how we can amend our Constitution to best structure, conduct, and finance our political process to properly govern ourselves. Then we must convince our state legislatures to call for a Constitutional Convention to either enact The Democracy Amendments proposed here, or something similar that will better accomplish the task. Our goal should be to provide equality of representation for all of us: libertarians, conservatives, moderates, liberals, progressives and independents.

I hope this book will assist that task.

In it, I propose a vision of how this might be done. Collectively, I refer to the several specific, inter-related amendment parts as "The Democracy Amendments."

Most parts of The Democracy Amendments have been proposed and discussed for many years. For this reason, when I discuss them in more detail, I liberally quote from those entities and individuals who are their strong proponents. Historically, most parts have been discussed separately, or only in conjunction with a few others. There is much risk in this approach. Most current amendment proposals would just fix a part in a way that would not resolve the underlying real problems that are distorting proper representation of our collective citizen interests.

With The Democracy Amendments, I've worked to correct this. Let's comprehensively reform the way we currently structure and finance our political system, in order to truly provide appropriate equality of representation for all.

I hope this book provokes much discussion and debate about which of the several alternative Constitutional Amendment proposals will be most effective. As we listen to the arguments and weigh the merits of various proposals, let's question what reform it is that we really need, and which proposal, or proposals, will best achieve it.

Let those organizations and individuals proposing Constitutional Amendment language limited to only a few purposes explain why that approach would be more effective than a much more comprehensive approach such as proposed with The Democracy Amendments. Let those pressuring Congress to initiate a 28th Amendment explain why Congress would ever initiate an amendment as broad and comprehensive as could be proposed by citizens directly through their state legislatures. Let those arguing against an Article V Convention initiated through our state leg-islatures explain why, as Congress fails to act, we citizens should continue to incur all the problems of our present political system without comprehensive reform. Finally, let those of us proposing much more comprehensive amend-ment reform through our state legislatures explain why the need for reform and its benefits are more important than the worries and concerns raised by having an Article V Convention.

PART I
The Democracy Amendments

A. One Comprehensive Amendment or Many Separate Amendments?

Effectively reforming the way we govern ourselves requires many inter-related parts.

If each separate part of reform is proposed as a separate amendment, at least ten separate amendments might be needed. If one or more of these amendments fails being adopted, the effectiveness of several other amendments could be jeopardized. For that reason, incorporating all required parts into a single comprehensive amendment that then can be subsequently submitted to each of the 50 states for ratification seems more likely to produce an effective result.

Such a complete proposed amendment is presented below, together with each of its parts, referred to therein as sections.

B. 28th Amendment Wording — The Democracy Amendments

Proposing an Amendment to the Constitution of the United States in order to: improve the way we elect our representatives; provide Congress with increased incentives to properly represent, legislate and govern in the broad public interests of all citizens; and to conduct and finance our elections, in a manner that prioritizes the broad public interests of citizens above the narrower interests of candidates, political parties, and special interests, so as to enhance the way we the people govern ourselves.

RIGHT TO VOTE: Section 1. *Every citizen of the United States, who is of legal voting age, shall have the fundamental right to vote in any public election held in the jurisdiction in which the citizen resides.*

CITIZEN ELECTION COMMISSIONS: Section 2. *Congress and each State shall establish Citizen Election Commissions to regulate and maintain the integrity and fairness of the election process on behalf of voters, each of which shall have a majority of members who are not current or recent legislators or members of any political party, and all members shall conduct its affairs in order to be independent from legislative and political party influence.*

CITIZEN FINANCING: Section 3. *All federal elections for Senator, Representative, President and Vice*

President, shall be publicly financed in a manner that, in major part, provides each registered voter in each primary and general election with an equal amount of monetary value from the federal treasury to be allocated among the primary and general election candidates as each registered voter sees fit.

CITIZEN REDISTRICTING: Section 4. *Each State's Citizen Election Commission shall conduct the periodic redrawing of voting district lines in an open and transparent process so as to produce districts that comply with U.S. Constitutional and Statute law and are independent from legislative and political party influence.*

NONPARTISAN BLANKET PRIMARIES: Section 5. *All primary elections in each state for President, Vice-President, Senator and Representative shall be conducted as nonpartisan blanket primaries, including all qualified candidates, regardless of party, with each registered voter entitled to participate, regardless of political party affiliation, using a form of ranked voting so as to result in the selection of two candidates for voters to choose among in the general election.*

MAJORITY VOTING: Section 6. *All general elections for President, Vice President and each U.S. Senator and U.S. Representative shall be conducted so that each winner shall only be elected by a majority of more than half of all the votes cast by registered voters.*

USE OF PUBLIC AIRWAVES AND DIGITAL NETWORKS: Section 7. *All elections for President, Vice President and all Senators and Representatives shall be conducted with the benefit of free use of the public airways and public digital networks for the purposes of moderated public debates, in-depth interviews with* *candidates, equal candidate presentations about their background, positions on issues and fitness for elected office, and coverage of the election process shall occur in a manner that provides ample and sufficient opportunity to inform and benefit all potential voters.*

SHORTER ELECTION CYCLES: Section 8. *All elections for President, Vice-President, and all Senators and Representatives shall begin and end within a period of no more than twelve, consecutive months.*

FULL DISCLOSURE: Section 9. *All campaign funding and expenditures related to all candidates for President, Vice President and all Senators and Representatives shall be promptly and publically disclosed in a timely manner that shall benefit all registered voters in making their decisions among the candidates prior to the election.*

ENCOURAGING VOTING AND REDUCING FRAUD AND MISTAKES: Section 10. *The Federal Citizens Election Commission shall, in a manner that is open and transparent and independent from legislative and political party influence, establish uniform times, standards and procedures for holding and conducting federal elections in the several states, and also regulate and enforce the campaign behavior and financing of all federal elections for President, Senators and Representatives so as to equally empower voters, encourage maximum voter turnout, prevent fraud, and prevent any regional or local advantage over election outcomes. Each State Citizen Election Commission shall regulate the times, places and manner of holding elections in their state in a manner that is consistent with U.S. Constitutional and Statute law as well as standards and procedures set by the Federal Citizens Election Commission.*

ENFORCEMENT: Section 11. *The Congress and the several States shall have concurrent power to implement in a timely manner and enforce the provisions of this article by appropriate legislation, provided that the States shall not abridge uniform federal standards set to enhance the integrity and fairness of the election process on behalf of all voters.*

OPERABILITY: Section 12. *This article shall be inoperative unless it shall have been ratified as an amendment to the Constitution by the legislatures of three fourths of the several states, or by conventions in the several States, as provided by Article V in the Constitution.*

As an alternative to the above, I've also included The Democracy Amendments as ten separate amendments in Appendix B. Assuming all 10 amendments were adopted and properly ratified, the same reforms would occur as with the single, more comprehensive amendment just presented.

PART II
A Vision of What Can Be

A Vision of What Can Be

Envision a time several or more years from now. *The Democracy Amendments* to our U.S. Constitution have been proposed and ratified by at least 38 states. Related enabling laws have also been enacted by Congress as well as by the legislatures of each of our 50 states. They are now part of the law by which we govern ourselves.

It's the beginning of our federal election cycle, at the end of which each of us will ultimately choose our next U.S. President, our state's next U.S. Senator if his or her term is ending, and our Representative to Congress. Let's consider how different the election process will be structured and funded, as compared to today.

Every citizen of legal voting age now has a constitutionally protected *right to vote,* where they reside, in the upcoming primary and general election. Previously this did not exist, which meant our electoral system was divided into 50 states, further subdivided into more than 3,000 counties and approximately 13,000 voting districts,[6] each separate from, and sometimes equal to, the others. In the past these differences have led to contradictory policies regarding ballot design, and denial of the right of soldiers on active duty, felons, and of students to vote. This correction now allows substantial numbers of citizens to properly exercise their right to vote.

No longer is gerrymandering of election districts to favor

either Democratic or Republican candidates the norm, depending on which party has predominant power in their state legislature. Instead *Citizen Election Commissions* ensure election districts are periodically redrawn in a non-partisan basis in accordance with legal principles outlined by our constitution and statutes as interpreted by our courts.

Citizen Election Commissions, at the federal level and in each state, now regulate the election process in accordance with The Democracy Amendments and enabling legislation at both the federal level and in each state. With more citizens involved who have no affiliation with any specific political party, and are also not candidates, the focus of the commissions is now redirected toward making the election process better serve the interests of all citizens. No longer is the process heavily influenced to best serve the interests of any one political party over the broader interests of all citizens.

As we choose our leaders, The Democracy Amendments will ensure we will have a good range of candidates to choose among, even though we obviously won't like them all. With public use of the airways during designated election periods there will be many more debates carried on radio and television with neutral moderators conducting the debates to best serve citizens rather than to serve a particular political party or network. Thus we'll be able to see, hear, and learn more in depth about each candidate's personal and professional background, their positions on important issues, how they present and defend these positions, and how they handle themselves under pressure in debates. Then we can more intelligently make up our minds.

Gone are the days when the two major political parties and

the major television networks were able to negotiate the number, scheduling, and format of debates to suit their best collective interests, at times by limiting or denying debate access to certain candidates.

For example, certain leaders of the Democratic National Committee (DNC) deliberately limited the number of debates in the fall of 2015 in order to favor better-known Hillary Clinton over less well-known candidates like Bernie Sanders and Martin O'Malley. In addition, the DNC manipulated the rules in order to completely deny Democratic presidential candidate Lawrence Lessig any participation in the debates. Lessig's positions on many aspects of these Democracy Amendments were attractive enough for him to raise significantly more money from a far greater number of supporters than either candidate Lincoln Chaffee or Jim Webb, both of whom were allowed into the debates. The DNC was effectively pre-selecting the candidates among whom we voters then get to choose.

Now the process is set to better serve our interests as citizens. If candidates are strongly supported with small contributions in the early stages of the primary election process by those voters who know them and their positions, they won't be denied participation in the debates, where far more voters can learn about, evaluate and chose whether to support them or not.

Elections now are financed with *citizen public funding* due to The Democracy Amendments. Thus, you and I and each registered voter now will receive an equal amount of monetary value, perhaps $50 — most likely in voucher form, which each of us can allocate among our preferred candidates for Representative, Senator or President. Gone are the days when the Supreme Court could interpret the first amendment in ways that enable campaigns to be funded primarily by the tiniest percentage of the wealthiest among us. These interpretations regularly resulted in Congress and the Executive branch enacting law and policy that favored the interests of those wealthy funders to the detriment of most of the rest of us. Now that financing has been democratized, candidates must be attractive to large numbers of voters in order to finance their campaigns. The voters will now have much more power to influence election outcomes, and candidates will have increased incentives to more broadly align their views on issues with the view of the majority of voters, and once in office, to enact law and policy to better serve the broad interests of all voters.

All primaries are now conducted as "*nonpartisan blanket primaries*" where 100 percent of all registered voters, regardless of party, may cast their ballots. Each political party may offer as many candidates as it likes, and anyone else may also enter as a candidate regardless of party, provided that each candidate must show sufficient support, most likely in the form of small donations. Gone are the "closed primaries," conducted separately by both the Democratic and Republican parties, where as little as 10-15 percent of all registered voters select the candidates all the rest of us must choose among in the general election.

Before The Democracy Amendments were enacted, candidates framed and presented their positions on issues primarily to that small percentage of voters they needed to please in order to successfully win in closed primary elections. This left out the many voters who don't closely identify with the candidates of either the Republican or Democratic parties. These voters have had no part in selecting the primary candidates they would prefer to choose among subsequently in the general election.

Now that 100 percent of registered voters can vote in the primary, candidates must consider how to differently present their positions on issues in ways that appeal much more broadly among voters. This should help rectify the situation we have today where, for example, a majority of all voters nationally can be in favor of sensible restrictions on gun use and ownership, but their views can effectively be blocked by candidates appealing only to a minority of voters in closed primaries.

As we vote in *nonpartisan blanket primaries*, we will now *rank* our preference for as many of the primary candidates on the ballot as we choose. This will help to ensure that only the two candidates preferred by the most of us will then compete in the general election.

General elections will now be conducted with *majority voting*, so the winning candidate can be elected only by a majority of more than half of all the votes cast. Gone are the days where, with several general election candidates and plurality voting, we often elected someone with only thirty or forty some percent of us in favor, and with a majority of voters having withheld their support. This should help whomever we elect to govern more effectively. In addition, to be successfully elected, candidates will need to ensure their positions on issues are better aligned with preferences held by the majority of voters. This should also help our elected leaders to work more effectively together, since the positions they espoused to get elected are likely to be less extreme than formerly occurred due to gerrymandering coupled with closed primaries.

All of the above improvements should allow us to have *shorter election cycles*. Most of us will certainly appreciate that! With a more open, inclusive, and competitive process with more equal opportunity for voters to get to know candidates, it should be less important for candidates to have previously been either a celebrity or long time politician in order to have broad name recognition before becoming a candidate. From now on, all candidates who demonstrate substantial support from those voters they've been able to reach, will have the opportunity for voters more broadly to learn about them in roughly equal measure through frequent appearances and debates on television, radio, and in other media. Thus it should be less important to have a longer campaign period in order to establish sufficient name recognition.

We voters will now also have quicker and broader *full disclosure* about how each campaign is funded and how it spends its money. The newly reconstituted *Citizen Election Commissions* have strengthened requirements relating to this reporting and now are much more aggressively enforcing rules in the event candidates fail to follow them. Gone are the days when, due to the bipartisan structure as established by Congress, its 3 Democratic and 3 Republican members repeatedly could not agree to take any substantive action on many enforcement issues. Every time they stalemated, the integrity of our political process was further undermined as abuses continued. Now, independent citizens have been added to each commission, thus avoiding stalemates. In addition they are charged with addressing issues to best serve citizens and preserve the integrity of the political process.

Citizen Election Commissions have also improved and strengthened requirements relating to voting rights and elections in many ways. Among other improvements there are now:

- Modernized on-line electronic voter registration procedures using proven technology to allow citizens to both register online and look up their voter registration information, thus ensuring that every eligible citizen can become and stay a registered voter.

- Procedures to ensure portability of registration to allow voters to easily and immediately update residence information when they move.

- Millions more voters able to register due to right-to-vote and registration improvements.

- Uniform requirements to inform voters of certain pending voting changes.

- Accelerated ways for lawyers to halt discriminatory election measures before they can harm citizens.

- Observers to monitor elections to ensure compliance with laws protecting the rights of Americans who speak limited English.

- Minimum early voting periods to make voting more accessible for everyone and provide a safety valve against Election Day overload.

- Minimum standards for voting, including voting machines, polling places, and resource allocation, all to improve the likelihood that voters will reliably be able to cast their vote and also to have it properly counted.

- Correction mechanisms that permit eligible citizens to correct errors on the voter rolls before and on Election Day, and therefore allow voters to cast a ballot that counts on Election Day.

The result of all these improvements due to the enactment of The Democracy Amendments is a rejuvenated political process in both the selection and election of candidates, and in the way our government functions. This will make equality of representation for all U.S. citizens much more likely in a Congress chosen and operating as required by The Democracy Amendments.

These changes increase the likelihood that Congress will finally begin to resolve such long standing issues as: ensuring the solvency and continuation of Social Security, providing good health care to all at the least total system-wide cost and in a sustainable manner over time, simplifying our federal tax code, creating a federal living wage, preserving our right to own and bear arms while sensibly regulating their use and safety, and sensibly addressing our national debt.

Moreover, Congress will now have increased incentive to re-consider laws that currently confer special economic benefit on specific industrial sectors and businesses while systematically transferring money from citizen pockets into the pockets of those sectors and businesses. The savings to citizens should exceed by many times the costs of citizen financing of our election process, thus providing a huge return on investment for citizens from enacting The Democracy Amendments.

PART III
Each Amendment in More Depth

1. Right to Vote

Voting is the foundation of our democracy. As such, it should be protected, promoted, and practiced. Yet our U.S. Constitution provides no explicit right to vote. This allows politicians in various states and jurisdictions to treat voting rights of citizens differently, and in many cases unequally. The result is, some citizens have fewer rights than others. It's time to rectify this with a uniform right to vote amendment.

Many different organizations and individuals support an explicit right to vote. Among them, the non-partisan, non-profit organization Fair Vote seeks to make democracy fair, functional, and fully representative.[7] Fair Vote describes itself as follows:

> "More than a decade ago, FairVote became the leading institutional voice calling for the establishment of an explicit individual right to vote in the U.S. Constitution. We believe that a grassroots movement to establish such an amendment would go a long way in ending the "voting wars" that plague us today. FairVote continues to serve as a trusted resource in support of activists, organizations, and elected officials working toward a right to vote amendment. Through our Promote Our Vote project, we work to build widespread support for a right to vote amendment, while advocating for pro-suffrage innovations at the local level."[8]

The Right to Vote part of The Democracy Amendments uses wording proposed by Fair Vote.

RIGHT TO VOTE: Section 1. Every citizen of the United States, who is of legal voting age, shall have the fundamental right to vote in any public election held in the jurisdiction in which the citizen resides."[9]

Why We Need a Right to Vote Amendment

As explained by Fair Vote:

"Enshrining an explicit right to vote in the Constitution would guarantee the voting rights of every citizen of voting age, ensure that every vote is counted correctly, and defend against attempts to enfranchise ineligible voters and disenfranchise eligible voters. It would empower Congress to enact minimum electoral standards to guarantee a higher degree of legitimacy, inclusivity, and consistency across the nation, and give our courts the authority to keep politicians in check when they try to game the vote for partisan reasons."[10]

"States protect the right to vote to different degrees based on the state's constitutional language and statutes. The federal government traditionally only steps in to prevent certain broad abuses, such as denying the right to vote based on race (15th Amendment), sex (19th Amendment), or age (26th Amendment)."[11]

"In most states, counties design their own ballots, pursue their own voter education, have their own policies for handling overseas ballots, hire and train their own poll workers, select polling place locations, and maintain their own voter registration lists. States have wide leeway in determining policies on absentee voting, polling hours and funding of elections. As a result, voters and potential voters have different experiences going

through the registration and voting process depending on where they live. These differences can be even more pronounced in some local elections because of varying degrees of federal and state support.[12]

"States also currently have the power to explicitly limit the franchise. Current data shows states have chosen to deny nearly six million American citizens the right to vote because of felony convictions, including millions who have completely paid their debt to society. Some states even deny certain classes of overseas voters the right to vote."[13]

This "amendment only ensures states meet certain clear standards in how they protect the right to vote. By ensuring that every American has an individual right to vote that is protected by the Constitution, this amendment establishes voting as an individual right, not just a privilege given by the states."[14]

Don't Citizens Have a Right to Vote in Presidential Elections?

As Explained by Fair Vote:

> "Not necessarily. Article II of the Constitution reads in part: "Each state shall appoint, such manner as the legislature thereof may direct, a number of electors…" In other words, it is the state legislature and not the citizens of a particular state that determine which presidential candidate receives that state's electoral votes. In the early decades of the country, several state legislatures actually appointed electors to the Electoral College, rather than hold popular elections in their state. In the 2000 Bush v. Gore decision, five justices declared, "The individual citizen has no federal constitutional right to vote for electors for the President of the United States unless and until the state legislature chooses a statewide election as the means to implement its power to appoint members of the Electoral College." The Court went on to say that Florida's legislature has the power to take that power away from the people at any time, regardless of the popular vote tally.

> "In addition, it took a constitutional amendment in 1961 to enable residents of Washington, D.C. to vote for president. But the millions of American citizens living in territories like Puerto Rico, the Virgin Islands, and Guam still cannot vote for president."[15]

2. Citizen Election Commissions

Citizens have relatively little say in how our political process is structured and managed today. Thus our biggest challenge is to restructure our political process to correct this. Having a Citizen Election Commission with impartial commissioners at the federal level and in each state is an important part of The Democracy Amendments as stated below.

> *CITIZEN ELECTION COMMISSIONS: Section 2.*
> *Congress and each State shall establish Citizen Election Commissions to regulate and maintain the integrity and fairness of the election process on behalf of voters, each of which shall have a majority of members who are not current or recent legislators or members of any political party, and all members shall conduct its affairs in order to be independent from legislative and political party influence.*

Selection of Commission Members

All commission members, at the federal level and in each of the 50 states, must be selected to meet the criteria as stated in The Democracy Amendments relating to Citizen Election Commissions. This includes a majority of the members of each commission who are not current or recent legislators or members of any political party. In addition all commission members shall conduct the affairs of each commission in order to be independent from legislative and political party influence.

The determination process as to the total number of commission members, their qualifications, and their exact selection process to become commissioners will be at the federal level debated and decided by Congress, and in each state by their respective legislatures. This will allow flexibility as to how best to meet to standards required by The Democracy Amendments.

One possible hypothetical approach is to assume a total of 12 commission members to be selected, and then to publically advertise the selection process and invite applicants to submit their applications online. Applicants would need to affirm that they meet all the qualifications established and that they did not have a conflict of interest. All applicants meeting these first criteria would then be invited to submit a supplemental application online in which they provided written responses to specific questions designed to give evaluators insight into their professional experience, reasons for wanting to serve on the Commission, and understanding and agreement with core standards of The Democracy Amendments, and any added statutory requirements.

Responses submitted by applicants might be reviewed, for example, on the federal level by selected members of the U.S. Government Accountability Office, and in each state by their equivalent state Office of Auditor, who would select a large number (perhaps 120) of the most qualified applicants to be interviewed. These applicants might be divided into 3 sub-pools: 30 Democrats, 30 Republicans, and 60 who are independent of either party. Following the interviews, the total pool might be reduced to 60, with 15

Democrats, 15 Republicans and 30 independents. These 60 might then be sent to the leaders of both divisions of, at the federal level, Congress, or in each state, the legislature, who would be entitled to remove up to 5 Democrats, 5 Republicans and 10 independents from the pool. From the remaining pool of 40, at the federal level the Comptroller General, and in each state, the Auditor, would draw the final 12 commission members by randomly drawing 3 names from the Democratic pool, 3 from the Republican pool, and 6 from the pool of independents.

The above hypothetical approach is somewhat similar to the way the California Citizen's Redistricting Commission selects its members.[16]

Duties of the Federal Citizens Election Commission

Specific duties of The Federal Citizens Election Commission would be debated and then established by Congress. However, as a minimum, these duties should include the following requirements as set forth in The Democracy Amendments:

- Power to regulate and enforce the *Right to Vote*.
- Power to regulate and maintain the integrity and fairness of the election process on behalf of voters.
- Power to regulate and maintain the integrity and fairness of *Citizen Financing* of all elections for President, Vice President, U.S. Senator and U.S. Representative.
- Power to regulate and maintain the integrity and fairness of *Nonpartisan Blanket Primaries* in all primary elections for President, Vice President, U.S. Senator and U.S. Representative.

- Power to regulate and maintain the integrity and fairness of voting, prevent fraud, and to establish uniform procedures related to the election process in both the primary and general elections for President, Vice President, U.S. Senator and U.S. Representative.

- Power, in conjunction with the Federal Communications Commission, to regulate and maintain the *Use of the Public Airways and Digital Networks* to schedule ample opportunity for citizens during each election cycle to learn about candidates, their backgrounds, skills, and ability to present and debate their positions on issues through frequent debates, using neutral moderators and formats designed to be best for voters, rather than for any particular political party or candidate.

- Power to regulate the length of the election cycle and significantly shorten it through *Use of the Public Airways and Digital Networks*.

- Power to regulate and mandate the manner and timing of *Full Disclosure* of all campaign funding and expenditures related to each candidate so this information is easily available to voters in a timely manner.

3. Citizen Financed Elections

At the heart of these Democracy Amendments is the need to restructure the way we finance the election process to give our political leaders much more incentive to serve the broad interests of all their constituents.

Results of Our Present System

Currently, the way we finance our political process produces the exact opposite result. Campaign funding comes from a tiny fraction of Americans, as recently described by Professor Lawrence Lessig and based on data from OpenSecrets.org:[17]

> "In 2014, 5.4 million Americans gave at least something to any congressional campaign or political party or PAC. That's about 1.75 percent of America."
>
> '.2 percent (610,000) of the contributors gave as much as 66 percent of the contributors.'
>
> .04 percent (122,000) gave the equivalent of the maximum allowed in one election — $2,600.'
>
> 'About a fifth as many — 26,000 or .008 percent — gave at least $10,000 to any set of candidates."

It's politicians' dependence on these few funders that gives most of them incentive to "lean to the green" in enacting, or sometimes obstructing, law, regulation, and policy in Washington toward the interests of this tiny proportion of funders. This in turn produces the result recently documented by Princeton professor Martin Gilens;[18] that in recent decades, whenever U.S. government policy preferences held by the top 10% of U.S. income earners DIFFER from the preferences of the remaining 90% of us (i.e. middle and lower classes), government policy outcomes bear essentially ZERO (statistically insignificant) correlation with the preferences of the 90% of us.

All this equates to improper representation. We declared our independence from Great Britain, fought a war, and founded our country largely over this issue. That's why correcting it is the paramount issue of our time, for it goes to the very heart of our democracy and representation.[19]

Election Advantages of Citizen Based Financing

The following part of The Democracy Amendments changes the financing of our political process to accomplish several advantages:

> *CITIZEN FINANCING: Section 3. All federal elections for Senator, Representative, President and Vice President, shall be publicly financed in a manner that, in major part, provides each registered voter in each primary and general election with an equal amount of monetary value from the federal treasury to be allocated among the primary and general election candidates as each registered voter sees fit.*

First, providing each registered voter with an equal amount of monetary value from the federal treasury and empowering each voter to allocate it among candidates is likely to dramatically increase voter participation. Since each voter must then decide how to "spend" this monetary value among the various candidates running for office, it creates a positive incentive for voters to become much more involved in learning about candidates and deciding whom to support.

Second, since candidates must receive support in small individual amounts from large numbers of registered voters in order to become viable and to qualify to participate in the many debates on the public airways, candidates have a powerful incentive to pay attention to the interests of these voters. Politicians thus become much more "dependent on the people alone," as the Framers of our Constitution originally intended[20].

Third, requiring prospective candidates to demonstrate their appeal to large numbers of voters willing to give them small individual amounts of campaign cash will dramatically level the playing field for all, and place the emphasis where it should be for a candidate, as opposed to our current system which distorts this concept by placing much emphasis on two less directly related factors:

- Poll numbers — Using poll numbers helps candidates who are already well known, for example, politicians, celebrities, sports figures, media hosts, and actors. Such candidates should nevertheless be required to demonstrate that they initially have the actual support of large numbers of voters willing to give them small donations.

- Large amounts of campaign cash — Self-funded wealthy candidates, or candidates supported by a small number of very wealthy campaign funders, are often treated as very viable today. Such candidates should also be required to demonstrate that they initially have the actual support of large numbers of voters willing to give them small donations to be viable.

Little consideration is currently given as to how the present process serves us best as citizens and voters. But if candidates have a sufficiently important message that strongly appeals to those supporters who have actually heard them, it's important that these candidates then have the opportunity for much larger numbers of voters to learn about them and decide for themselves whether they do or don't like them. If such candidates are denied the opportunity to participate in the debates, it's likely to be fatal to their candidacy. Larger numbers of voters will never get the opportunity to learn about them.

Such distorted outcomes were especially evident in the 2016 Democratic Presidential primary race.

Two Examples

Hillary Clinton entered the race being much better known than Bernie Sanders. Hillary had a strong national following, while Bernie was relatively much less widely known. Candidate Clinton had already been First Lady for 8 years when her husband was President. In addition she had been a U.S. Senator from New York and a Secretary of State for 4 years. In comparison, Bernie Sanders had only been Mayor of Burlington, a Vermont U.S. Congressman for 16 years, and U.S. Senator since 2006.

Hillary also had another big advantage. Congresswoman Debbie Wasserman-Schultz was co-chair of Hillary's campaign committee during her unsuccessful run for president in 2008. It appears that Wasserman-Schultz and other similarly minded members of the Democratic National Committee hoped that by reducing the number of debates, having a single network primarily responsible for hosting each one, and by scheduling the debates opposite other events that would draw some potential viewers away, Hillary might remain better known than the other candidates.

This strategy was designed to help Hillary emerge from the shortened debate structure as the dominant candidate, thus avoiding what happened in 2008 when, as more and more voters learned about Barack Obama, his standing in the polls rose dramatically, with Hillary ultimately losing the Democratic Party nomination.

Back in March of 2015, poll numbers placed Bernie Sanders in only the low single digits while Hillary Clinton polled over 50 points higher. But even with the much more limited debate format, as more and more voters listened to Bernie and to Hillary in the debates and media, Bernie's poll numbers rose dramatically.

Compare that result to the treatment of another Democratic candidate for President, Lawrence Lessig, a Harvard professor who passionately believes that fixing our democracy can't wait. As expressed on his campaign website,[21] Lessig believes that:

> "Again and again, what America wants, Congress doesn't do — because the citizens who fund elections are represented, and the rest of us are not."

> 'Every issue — from climate change to gun safety, from Wall Street reform to defense spending — is blocked by this fundamental problem: Congress does not represent the people.'

> 'The solution is to fix our democracy. First!'

Candidate Lessig had written about these issues in a book, *Republic Lost*, with good reviews, given two widely viewed TED talks, and delivered over 200 well-received presentations across America on the need, and ways, to fix our democracy. He'd also organized the so-called New Hampshire Rebellion to try to inject this issue into the NH presidential primary debates, and founded Mayday PAC to raise money to support U.S. House and Senate candidates willing to champion this issue.

In the first Democratic debate for President, on October 13th, 2015, five candidates participated: Hillary Clinton, Bernie Sanders, Martin OMalley, Lincoln Chaffee and Jim Webb. Lawrence Lessig was not included. Why?

Understanding why candidate Lessig was not included, when the others were, illustrates much of what is wrong with the way we currently structure and fund elections as part of our political process, and why citizen financed elections would much better serve the interests of us all.

Hillary Clinton announced her candidacy in mid-April, 2015, and Bernie Sanders and Martin O'Malley announced in late May.

By September 30th, 2015, all candidates for president were required by the Federal Election Commission to report their respective amounts of campaign contributions and expenditures. Hillary Clinton and Bernie Sanders had both raised significant amounts of campaign money — Hillary over $77 million and Bernie over $41 million. Martin O'Malley had raised about $3.3 million.[22] Thus these were, at the time, clearly the front-runners.

Let's compare these leading candidates with three others: Lawrence Lessig, Lincoln Chafee, and Jim Webb. Of the three, only Chafee and Webb were included in the first debate.

- Lincoln Chafee declared his candidacy on June 3rd, 2015 and by September 30th, 2015, immediately prior to the first debate, had received $408,201, of which $363,000 consisted of loans to his campaign.[23] Lincoln had very few supporter donors when compared to many other candidates.

- Jim Webb declared his candidacy on July 2nd, 2015

and by September 30th, 2015, had received $696,972, none of which were loans.[24] Compared to candidate Lincoln Chaffee, Jim Webb had more supporter donors and raised more money.

- Lawrence Lessig filed considerably later, on August 11th, 2015, for an exploratory committee, and said he'd consider being a candidate, but *only* if he was able to raise more than $1 million dollars from a large number of supporters by Labor Day to demonstrate his viability as a candidate. He accomplished this in only 4 weeks with contributions from about 10,000 individuals and also met the qualifications for federal matching funds. By September 30th, 2015 Lessig reported $1,016,189, of which he had loaned his campaign only $629.[25]

One might think that if Lessig, or any other presidential candidate for that matter, can generate this much enthusiastic support, in this short time, from the relatively small number of American voters who have heard of him, or her, a sensible citizen-focused primary candidate selection process should afford such candidates the opportunity to reach voters who haven't yet heard about them. Only then can larger number of voters learn about them and decide if they like them and their ideas.

Apparently Debbie Wasserman-Schultz and certain other leaders of the Democratic National Committee didn't think so. The DNC, together with the TV network for the first debate, had decided that raising large amounts of contributions quickly from a good proportion of the of the people who actually did know about a candidate early on in the campaign wasn't a criteria they'd use for participation in the debates. Instead, the DNC wanted candidates for the debate to have been selected by at least 1% in each of 3 national polls conducted in the 6 weeks prior to the first debate. Since 1% in a national poll is expected to be representative of 1% of the sample population, this is the equivalent of 2,189,590 of Americans that are eligible to vote[26] or 1,463,110 of registered voters[27] already knowing enough about a recently announced candidate to decide to select them, before they've even had the chance to learn more about them in a nationally televised debate. Is this reasonable?

Because both Lincoln Chafee and Jim Webb had announced early, their names had been repeatedly mentioned in the media for several months before the polls. Lawrence Lessig, having announced much later, had no such name recognition advantage, despite the fact that he had raised much more in campaign contributions from a much greater number of supporters than either Chafee or Webb. Yet Chafee and Webb both met the DNC standard and were both invited to the first debate, while Lessig was excluded.

Moreover, Wasserman-Schultz and many others at the DNC portrayed Lessig as a single-issue candidate and quietly lobbied to keep his name from being included in the presidential candidate preference polls conducted prior to upcoming first debate. Consequently, Lessig's name wasn't even included as one of the democratic candidates to choose among for 7 of the 10 remaining polls the DNC considered as appropriate prior to the first debate on October 13th. Thus Lessig missed the opportunity to reach a much broader audience. Subsequently some of these same DNC leaders specifically requested Iowa Democratic party leaders not to invite him to their October 24th Jefferson Jackson dinner. This prevented Lessig from receiving another national opportunity to join other remaining Democratic Party candidates attending, since this event was also heavily reported in the media.

Meanwhile, before the next debate on November 14th

approached, Lessig's campaign had continued to gear up, hired staff with deep experience in national campaigns, contracted for media advertising in Iowa and New Hampshire, and contacted upcoming polling organizations about being included in the polls. All this was starting to get results. Despite relatively little media coverage, Lessig met or exceeded the 1% threshold in first one poll, and then another, and with only a couple of weeks to go, it became clear that Lessig would meet the polling standard of 1% in at least 3 polls in the 6 weeks prior to the November 14th debate.[28] So what did the DNC do? They changed the rules. The new rule said he could only participate if he had already received 1% in 3 polls that had all been conducted *prior to* 6 weeks before the debate. This meant Lessig would have had to finish qualifying prior to October 10th. In effect, the DNC said, "Larry, you weren't in the first debate. Thus we can't let you into any of the remaining debates."

Thus, with still over a year to go to the November, 2016 election, Larry Lessig's Presidential campaign effectively ended before he ever really got started, and before millions of Americans ever had the opportunity to get to fairly evaluate him.

Lest you think these actions are limited to the Democratic National Committee, or are personal to Lessig's candidacy, the same thing happened to Republican candidate for President Buddy Roemer in the 2012 Republican debates. Buddy ran on a "repair our democracy" platform, much as Lessig did, and Buddy Roemer was not invited to any of the Republican debates[29] [30] because he failed to meet the 2% minimum criterion, and when he met the 2% minimum criterion, CNN (the debate organizer) increased the minimum fundraising requirement needed to be admitted to the debate.[31] Roemer was also not included as an option in several polls.[32]

These are only two examples among many candidates who appear to have significant numbers of small donor supporters, but who are nevertheless denied the opportunity for more potential voters to hear about them in debates. This denial is directly related to the use of early polling numbers, coupled with an emphasis on the "total" campaign money received, regardless of whether most of it is provided by candidates themselves, as wealthy individuals, or by a small number of very wealthy campaign funders.

The DNC and RNC actions above are both good examples of what Professor Lessig refers to as "Tweedism". Boss Tweed is chiefly remembered for the cronyism of his Tammany Hall political machine a century and a half ago, through which he bilked the city of New York of massive sums of money.[33]

Such actions by the Democratic and Republican National Committees are an ugly reminder of Boss Tweed's infamous statement that *"I don't care who does the electing as long as I do the nominating."*[34]

Most of us probably think *deciding which candidates to nominate is **our** responsibility.*

Simply put, in the above examples, the DNC and the RNC are preselecting out the candidates you and I get to hear about, and therefore we don't get to choose among them in the primary election. But as the above examples show, that's what happens, given the way our political system is presently structured.

A Better Way to Determine Viable Candidates — With Citizen Based Financing

Pollsters, at the beginning of an election cycle, often ask us to decide who we like before many of us have had an opportunity to learn about most candidates. And the media often decide who's "viable" based on these early polls, plus the total amount of money a candidate has amassed, regardless of the number of people who donated. So our responses tend to favor those we have already heard of and the ones the media has deemed "viable". This gives candidates who are well known, for example politicians, celebrities, sports figures, media hosts and actors, an advantage in early polling.

However, we citizens likely benefit most from a quite different system, one that will provide us with a range of qualified candidates from whom to choose. We can accomplish this by providing to each registered voter in each primary and general election a specific amount of monetary value, for example - $50, from the federal treasury to be allocated among the primary and general election candidates as each voter sees fit. Using this method, once an individual has filed as a possible candidate, they must prove they are a "viable" candidate, and thus eligible to participate in a wide variety of public debates. Only then can they and their messages be exposed to much greater numbers of potential voters who may initially not know much about them. In order to prove they are viable, each candidate must receive a threshold number of small value contributions from citizens to show that their message and positions on issues have sufficient support.

Who sets the threshold level of support required of candidates?

What constitutes the proper threshold would be debated and ultimately decided by Congress and/or the federal Citizen Election Commission, who would then regulate to enable and enforce the enacted laws and regulations. The thresholds for U.S. Representative, Senator, and President are likely to be different; lower for U.S. Representative, more for Senator, and even more for President since there are significant differences in the number of registered voters and geography of voting area for each of these positions. Moreover, with regard to Senators, there are significant differences in size and population between states, so variations in the threshold may also need to be considered.

Currently, to register as a candidate for United States Representative, Senator, or President, it's only necessary to file a Statement of Candidacy with the Federal Elections Commission (F.E.C.) stating that the potential candidate has received contributions aggregating in excess of $5,000 or made expenditures aggregating in excess of $5,000[35].

In addition, a candidate for President must meet the age (35) and residency (14 years) requirements[36]. Because it's relatively easy to file, as of January 20th, 2015, some 1,500 candidates for the U.S. Presidential election had filed with the F.E.C.

Obviously, it would be quite unworkable for each of us to sort through and choose among all 1,500, which is why it's so important to have the requirement that each candidate prove their "viability" by having registered voters send them a sufficient number of small donations to meet the debate participation threshold. This should significantly reduce the field.

Once each candidate has registered by filing the required forms, he or she would automatically be eligible to receive small donations from registered voters. In addition each candidate would be given an opportunity to prepare and submit for posting on a public, central web site for each race, detailed information about their personal and professional background, and their positions on a wide variety of issues.

Candidates who qualify as viable would then have their information moved to a separate website. This would help the general public focus more easily on the candidates who have qualified as viable. All viable candidates would then be invited to participate in a broad range of many debates on TV and in other media, so that large numbers of voters could learn more detail about each of their personal and professional backgrounds, positions on issues, how they articulate those positions, and how well they hold up in debates. In turn, registered voters who view these debates will be able to indicate those they wish to support by means of allocating additional small donations to those candidates.

All Americans would quickly know which candidates are receiving the most money, as their receipts will be promptly disclosed by the federal Citizens Elections Commission. This approach should substantially reduce the need for candidate preference polling among the many candidates, since registered voters will have already indicated their preferences by means of the way they've chosen to allocate their small donations.

If it's necessary to further winnow the field in the latter stages of the debates, the federal Citizens Election Commission would use criteria, including the number and amount of small donations, to do so.

Currently, getting on the ballot is regulated by each state, and the timing and requirements vary, sometimes considerably. Usually it involves collecting certain numbers of petition signatures from properly registered voters. With The Democracy Amendments, the federal Citizens Election Commission will set uniform standards to be applied throughout all 50 states. Since registered voters will now have signified their support for certain candidates through allocation of their small donations, this should replace the current practice of collecting signatures to qualify for inclusion on the ballot in each state.

Can Candidates Still Receive Large Donations and/or Self Fund Themselves?

Yes, but it will still be the total number of donors that determines whether the candidate is viable. Just having a lot of money from a few donors will likely not meet the threshold requirement of viability for participation in public debates. And vastly improved disclosure will quickly make it clear to voters which candidates have broad public support instead of support from a smaller number of wealthy supporters, or from candidates self-funding with their own money.

How will Registered Voters Receive Funds to Allocate Among Candidates They Like?

Here's an example. At the beginning of each election cycle, each registered voter will receive a voucher in the form of a stored-value card — call it a pre-paid card if you prefer — of a certain amount, say $50, which that registered voter may allocate only among the candidates who have filed for U.S. Representative, Senator or President.

Alternatively, as part of a new national database of every registered voter, an online account for each voter could be created with the predetermined amount in it, which voters could then allocate much as with the stored-value card. The actual method and amount would be decided by the federal Citizen Election Commission. With experience and due to changing technology and costs, the actual amount and method will likely need to change over time. For example, there could be one card, or account, per registered voter, to be used for all federal races, or say 3 cards, or accounts, one for the U.S. Representative races, one for Senator, and one for President with different values per card since each type of race will be different in geography, cost and complexity. Regardless of which specific approach is chosen by the federal Citizens Election Committee, their underlying intent should be to allow this to be done in the way that gives the maximum number of registered voters incentive to become more knowledgeable about the candidates and to participate in the political process.

How Much Federal Money Will This Cost?

Total campaign costs rise with every election, and have historically been higher every 4 years when we chose a U.S. President in addition to our U.S. Representative, and (some years) our Senator. For the two year 2011-2012 election cycle, the total cost was about $6.3 billion[37].

If we divide this $6.3 billion by the number of U.S. registered voters (145,311,000),[38] the cost per registered voter in 2012 is about $43.36. Costs seem to go up every presidential election cycle, so a $50 voucher is likely to be roughly in the right range. However, other variables also apply.

Advertising is a large part of current campaign expenditures. This will dramatically change with The Democracy

Amendments, since now all television and other main media users of the public airways will be providing candidates with free access for large numbers of debates and other media events. In addition to leveling the playing field for candidates, this will dramatically lower candidate campaign costs and thus also lower the amount of federal money it will cost for citizen based financing.

Why Use Federal Money for Citizen Based Financing?

A common response from many of us, when considering the use of our federal tax dollars for citizen based campaign financing is: *"Why should I give my good money to that bad politician."* Obviously, we're not going to like them all equally. So why do it?

There are many reasons, but most importantly, because it will give all citizens a HUGE return on their public investment.

As previously discussed, about 98 percent of all U.S. citizens don't give any contributions at all to any federal candidate. Thus, until now candidates have had incentive to "lean to the green" to get contributions from a tiny percentage of the wealthiest amongst us, and therefore have been enacting laws, regulations, and policies which have been well documented to primarily serve their wealthy funders' interests, rather than the interests of 98 percent of us. This in turn, moves amazing amounts of money out of our pockets, and into theirs, in addition to distorting outcomes on many other issues in ways that adversely affect the 98 percent of us.

The total 2016 budget of the U.S. Government is approximately 4 trillion dollars[39], while the annualized total federal election cost in 2012 was only about 3.15 billion dollars.[40] Since we know that election costs rise rapidly with each subsequent presidential election cycle, let's increase the 3.15 billion to an estimated annual amount of $4 billion dollars in 2016.

This estimated $4 billion dollar per year cost of all federal campaigns in year 2016 is only a tiny fraction in relation to the 2016 total U.S. budget. In fact it's only one-tenth of one percent of the total, a figure so small that you and I could hardly even see it, if I presented it in either bar chart or pie chart format.

It's precisely for this reason that, without The Democracy Amendments, wealthy campaign funders have an incentive to contribute large amounts of campaign funding to political candidates. Imagine if you were a wealthy industrialist and with your campaign contributions you could tip just a modest part of the massive $4 trillion federal budget expenditures into your pocket, or at least into the pocket of your business. Or if you could tip a law in your company's direction that would allow you to charge higher prices to all U.S. consumers while protecting you from competition by others. What a huge return on your investment this could amount to. The dollars would flow in, millions or even billions of them, in relation to your initial payment of campaign contributions. It's exactly these type of actions that have corrupted our entire political system in Washington D.C. today.

By adopting The Democracy Amendments, to provide citizen-based financing of elections, we citizens can provide our elected federal politicians with a powerful incentive to enact laws, regulations, and policy that serve our interests.

Getting Citizens a Return on Our Investment in Campaigns?

Suppose I could offer you, and every American citizen, at reasonable risk, an investment that would likely double your money every year, now and into the foreseeable future. Each year you'd get your investment back, plus an equal sum as a return on your investment, and this would continue each year thereafter. Interested?

I'll bet you are! I can't invest my own money today and get a return anywhere near as good as this. A return of 100% a year, year after year, is a whopper of an investment.

Our normal ways to invest money produce much, much, lower returns. As I write this in 2016, if we invest in a savings or Certificate of Deposit account, we're likely to earn at most, about 2% annually. Investing long term in the stock market might bring us annual real earnings in the 4-10% range, and we're likely to average much closer to the lower number. In short, most of us can't even come close to an annual return of 100% or more. It's simply inconceivable.

So when I suggest that there's a way all American citizens can earn, with reasonable risk, an annual return of more than 100% now and into the foreseeable future, I bet you're suspicious. That's fair. We citizens should be careful in evaluating such proposals. But if The Democracy Amendments are adopted, and Congress and our federal politicians have incentive to pass laws, regulations, and policies to serve our interests as citizens, such returns are very possible, and likely.

All that's necessary is to reverse or tip federal laws, regulations and policy in our direction, to send these returns on investment our way rather than their way, as has been happening for many decades up until now.

There are many ways to do this, but consider just a few of the following examples. And remember, it only costs $4 billion dollars per year today, the annual equivalent of only about $12.50 per person[41], or about $36 per household[42] in 2016, to finance our entire federal election system.

Returns to Broadcasters, Rather than Citizens

In 1996, Congress decided to allocate for free an additional part of the public airways to existing television broadcasters so they could switch from analog to digital television.

Digital broadcasting brings not only a higher quality picture, like analog HDTV, but also the transmission of more information using the same amount of spectrum. While one channel of old analog signal can be sent on one 6-MHz channel of spectrum, up to six channels of new digital information could be sent over the same 6-MHz band of spectrum. This digital information can include not only television and radio signals, but also paging devices, cellular phones and computer data.

In other words, the digital technology multiplies the uses-and consequently, the economic value-of the existing spectrum. As then FCC Chairman Reed Hundt explained: It is a standard that potentially converts a town with six over-the-air channels into one with 60. And in addition to multiple TV channels, the standard allows broadcasters to transmit text and data — the local newspaper or brand new software — directly to the next generation of computer-powered TVs.

Government auctions for use of part of the public airways spectrum are routine these days for private companies wishing to make money by providing telecommunication services through use of the public airways for users of items such as cell phone and pagers. Such auctions regularly bring billions dollars into our federal treasury. Citizens otherwise would have to provide this money in taxes and user fees to balance the federal budget. This added allocation of the public airway spectrum was even more valuable to TV broadcasters, and they reached new highs in their

Congressional campaign contributions and lobbying efforts to secure it for free.

The Federal Communications Commission estimated that when Congress voted not to conduct this auction of rights for TV broadcasters, and instead give it away for free, it cost our federal treasury as much as $70 billion dollars[43] in 1997. That's over $600 per average American household that we had to make up in taxes and user fees to balance our federal budget. Said differently, by spending $4 billion dollars of our money as taxpayers for Citizen Funded Campaigns to give our representatives in Congress and the FEC incentive to put this out to bid, the resulting $70 billion dollars was enough, back in 1997, to finance our entire federal political process for over 17 years into the future!

Said differently, again, that's more than a 1,700 percent one-time return on our investment, from just this one example.

Increasing Profits of the Pharmaceutical Industry, at the Expense of All Citizens

U.S. Pharmaceutical companies have long been able to charge higher prices, whatever the market will bear, for their drugs in the United States due to patent protection laws. Meanwhile they market these same drugs to other countries at much lower prices, at whatever over their marginal cost they can negotiate. That's why prices for the same brand name drug in many other countries can be much lower than what we pay here in USA. Canadians pay an average of 40% less, France and Germany 50% less.[44]

However, it used to be legal for wholesalers of pharmaceutical drugs in other countries to purchase these U.S. brand name drugs at lower prices and then mark them up somewhat and sell them back into the American market at lower prices that those being charged for the same drugs by U.S pharmaceutical companies. This is simply engaging in free trade, which benefits consumers by lowering prices, much as our country does with all kinds of products in relation to other countries.

But in 1987, the pharmaceutical industry, with the help of large campaign contributions and much lobbying, convinced Congress to pass the Prescription Drug Marketing Act that, among other things, imposed a ban on re-importing prescription drugs from other countries, supposedly to protect Americans from bad drugs coming across our borders. Banning bad drugs is a legitimate issue for a certain portion of drugs coming from other countries that don't meet our standards. But not for a large portion which are either from reputable pharmaceutical firms overseas, or from similar U.S. firms that simply market their drugs (often in exactly the same packaging) to other countries at lower prices. Several other countries deal with this smaller problem of poor quality drugs by establishing an inspection and testing program at relatively low cost in relation to the potential savings to their country's consumers.

What Congress really did in 1987 was to ban free trade in pharmaceuticals from other countries. It's now illegal for you or me to purchase pharmaceuticals at much lower prices from, for example, Canada, or for a Canadian pharmaceutical wholesaler to sell drugs into our U.S. market at lower prices. The result is that since 1987 U.S. pharmaceutical industry profits have soared, and stayed that way for decades.

In 2014 total U.S. pharmaceutical sales were around $370 billion dollars.[45] If, by reversing this one 1987 law and allowing American consumers to purchase pharmaceuticals at lower prices from other countries, we only reduced total U.S. pharmaceutical sales by 10%, a very conservative estimate, this would result in pharmaceutical savings into the pockets of

Americans of about $37 billion dollars per year, and similar 10% savings would continue each and every year into the future.

By spending $4 billion dollars of our money as taxpayers for Citizen Funded Campaigns to give our representatives in Congress incentive to reverse this one law to serve our citizen interests, we collectively would receive $37 billion in year one and a similar, or slightly larger amount each year as drug prices continue to rise in the future. That's enough of a return to finance, every year, our entire federal political process for over 9 years into the future!

Said differently, that's more than a 900 percent per year return on our investment, from just this one example.

Cozying Up to Wall Street and the Financial Sector, at the Expense of All Citizens

For decades, the financial sector has outstripped all other sources of campaign contributions to federal candidates and parties. Insurance companies, securities and investment firms, real estate interests, and commercial banks provide the bulk of that money.[46] The sector regularly contributes large sums to both parties, though its giving tends to favor whichever party can be most helpful when laws, regulations, and policies are being considered that might adversely affect them.[47]

In return, candidates, both major political parties, most members of Congress, and relevant federal government agencies pay close attention to their respective interests. Members of Congress have become very adept at "leaning to the green" in structuring laws, and in working to ease government regulations and policy so as not to be too hard on them.

Banking industry donations and influence have a lot to do with why Congress supported bankruptcy reform legislation that made it easier for companies to enter bankruptcy to restructure, shed debt and usually emerge stronger and more competitive, while at the same time made it harder and harder for individuals to shed student loan debt. Insurance industry donations and influence explain why Congress never even seriously considered how to provide good quality health care to all Americans at the least system-wide cost, in a manner that's sustainable over time. This is despite the fact that most other developed countries manage to accomplish this in various ways at a smaller percentage of their GDP economic productivity and with better overall health outcomes than in our country. It explains why compensation received by hedge fund managers continues to be taxed at lower 20% capital gains rates rather than as salary that is ordinarily taxed at the 39.6% marginal income tax rates an average person would have to pay on such income.[48]

Remember the "New Democrats" rebranding of the Democratic Party beginning in the late 1980s and championed by Bill Clinton as he ran for President in 1992 and after the Republicans trounced the Democrats in the 1994 mid-term elections. A major part of this rebranding was to espouse policies more favorable to Wall Street. In short, Republicans were getting lots more campaign contributions from the financial sector, and the Democrats wanted in!

Subsequently, President Bill Clinton signed the Gramm-Leach-Bliley Act permitting the partial repeal of the Glass-Steagall Act, which since the 1930s had worked to separate lower risk commercial banking from much higher risk investment banking. While commentators argue about whether this action caused the great recession which followed in 2007–08, there is widespread agreement that relatively lax oversight by Congress and federal regulators during the 1980s and 90s helped to create the "irrationally exuberant" and complacent conditions that led financiers to improperly underestimate, sometimes by vast amounts, the amount of financial risk they were incurring, and that such actions greatly contributed to what followed after the Great Recession began at the very end of 2007.

Between the third quarter of 2007 and the first quarter of 2009, American households lost $13 trillion dollars of net worth.[49] If this amount were divided equally among all U.S. households, it is the equivalent of every household in America losing slightly over $115,000 of net worth.[50] In addition, approximately 8.7 million jobs were lost between February 2008 and February 2010. [51]

If we had spent $4 billion dollars a year of our tax money for Citizen Funded Campaigns, and given our representatives in Congress incentive to put citizen interests ahead of those of the financial sector, we could have avoided or even somewhat minimized the resulting loss of $13 trillion dollars of net worth and 8.7 million jobs. In this case, the return on investment for citizens, although incalculable, would with reasonable certainty, clearly be astounding!

And these are just a few of many, many more possible examples. Adopting Citizens Financed Elections as part of The Democracy Amendments is a very powerful part of comprehensively reforming the way we structure and finance our political process to properly serve the interests of all citizens.

4. Citizen Redistricting

Creating and managing voting districts in an impartial manner is another crucial part of The Democracy Amendments. They need to be drawn so as to represent the interests of all citizens, and not just to advantage one political party or candidate over another. Therefore, The Democracy Amendments includes the following provision:

CITIZEN REDISTRICTING: Section 4. Each State's Citizen Election Commission shall conduct the periodic redrawing of voting district lines in an open and transparent process so as to produce districts that comply with U.S. Constitutional and Statute law and are independent from legislative and political party influence

In the past, there have been a multitude of absurd examples of a political party in control of a state legislature using its influence to create crazily drawn districts that defy geographic and population integrity, but favor a particular political party or candidate. Unfortunately, this practice generally produces a winner whose views align more closely with voters within the crazily drawn district than with those of the general electorate in the vicinity of the district. This leads to a more polarized legislature that is more contentious, less inclined to compromise, and thus less likely to agree on budgets and many other important types of legislation that need to be regularly completed to serve the broad interests of most citizens.

In response to these problems, a growing number of states have in recent years made changes to their laws to ensure that the process of redistricting is more impartial, and accomplished in a manner that better serves the overall interests of its citizens. The largest, and therefore perhaps most relevant of these, is California. While each state will need to establish its own legal process to have its respective Citizen Election Commission redistrict in a manner that meets the new Constitutional mandate, let's use California as an example of how one state, in the absence of a Citizen Election Commission, has chosen to act with regard to its redistricting. Here's their law, which I quote in its entirety.

CALIFORNIA CONSTITUTION ARTICLE 21

REDISTRICTING OF SENATE, ASSEMBLY, CONGRESSIONAL AND BOARD OF EQUALIZATION DISTRICTS

SECTION 1. In the year following the year in which the national census is taken under the direction of Congress at the beginning of each decade, the Citizens Redistricting Commission described in Section 2 shall adjust the boundary lines of the congressional, State Senatorial, Assembly, and Board of Equalization districts (also known as "redistricting") in conformance with the standards and process set forth in Section 2.

CALIFORNIA CONSTITUTION ARTICLE 21

REDISTRICTING OF SENATE, ASSEMBLY, CONGRESSIONAL AND BOARD OF EQUALIZATION DISTRICTS

SEC. 2.

(a) The Citizens Redistricting Commission shall be created no later than December 31 in 2010, and in each year ending in the number zero thereafter.

(b) The commission shall:

(1) conduct an open and transparent process enabling full public consideration of and comment on the drawing of district lines;

(2) draw district lines according to the redistricting criteria specified in this article; and

(3) conduct themselves with integrity and fairness.

(c)

(1) The selection process is designed to produce a commission that is independent from legislative influence and reasonably representative of this State's diversity.

(2) The commission shall consist of 14 members, as follows: five who are registered with the largest political party in California based on registration, five who are registered with the second largest political party in California based on registration, and four who are not registered with either of the two largest political parties in California based on registration.

(3) Each commission member shall be a voter who has been continuously registered in Cal-

ifornia with the same political party or unaffiliated with a political party and who has not changed political party affiliation for five or more years immediately preceding the date of his or her appointment. Each commission member shall have voted in two of the last three statewide general elections immediately preceding his or her application.

(4) The term of office of each member of the commission expires upon the appointment of the first member of the succeeding commission.

(5) Nine members of the commission shall constitute a quorum. Nine or more affirmative votes shall be required for any official action. The four final redistricting maps must be approved by at least nine affirmative votes which must include at least three votes of members registered from each of the two largest political parties in California based on registration and three votes from members who are not registered with either of these two political parties.

(6) Each commission member shall apply this article in a manner that is impartial and that reinforces public confidence in the integrity of the redistricting process. A commission member shall be ineligible for a period of 10 years beginning from the date of appointment to hold elective public office at the federal, state, county, or city level in this State. A member of the commission shall be ineligible for a period of five years beginning from the date of ap-

pointment to hold appointive federal, state, or local public office, to serve as paid staff for, or as a paid consultant to, the Board of Equalization, the Congress, the Legislature, or any individual legislator, or to register as a federal, state or local lobbyist in this State.

(d) The commission shall establish single-member districts for the Senate, Assembly, Congress, and State Board of Equalization pursuant to a mapping process using the following criteria as set forth in the following order of priority:

(1) Districts shall comply with the United States Constitution. Congressional districts shall achieve population equality as nearly as is practicable, and Senatorial, Assembly, and State Board of Equalization districts shall have reasonably equal population with other districts for the same office, except where deviation is required to comply with the federal Voting Rights Act or allowable by law.

(2) Districts shall comply with the federal Voting Rights Act (42 U.S.C. Sec. 1971 and following).

(3) Districts shall be geographically contiguous.

(4) The geographic integrity of any city, county, city and county, local neighborhood, or local community of interest shall be respected in a manner that minimizes their division to the extent possible without violating the requirements of any of the preceding subdivisions. A

community of interest is a contiguous population which shares common social and economic interests that should be included within a single district for purposes of its effective and fair representation. Examples of such shared interests are those common to an urban area, a rural area, an industrial area, or an agricultural area, and those common to areas in which the people share similar living standards, use the same transportation facilities, have similar work opportunities, or have access to the same media of communication relevant to the election process. Communities of interest shall not include relationships with political parties, incumbents, or political candidates.

(5) To the extent practicable, and where this does not conflict with the criteria above, districts shall be drawn to encourage geographical compactness such that nearby areas of population are not bypassed for more distant population.

(6) To the extent practicable, and where this does not conflict with the criteria above, each Senate district shall be comprised of two whole, complete, and adjacent Assembly districts, and each Board of Equalization district shall be comprised of 10 whole, complete, and adjacent Senate districts.

(e) The place of residence of any incumbent or political candidate shall not be considered in the creation of a map. Districts shall not be drawn for the purpose of favoring or discriminating against an incumbent, political candidate, or political party.

(f) Districts for the Congress, Senate, Assembly, and State Board of Equalization shall be numbered consecutively commencing at the northern boundary of the State and ending at the southern boundary.

(g) By August 15 in 2011, and in each year ending in the number one thereafter, the commission shall approve four final maps that separately set forth the district boundary lines for the congressional, Senatorial, Assembly, and State Board of Equalization districts. Upon approval, the commission shall certify the four final maps to the Secretary of State.

(h) The commission shall issue, with each of the four final maps, a report that explains the basis on which the commission made its decisions in achieving compliance with the criteria listed in subdivision (d) and shall include definitions of the terms and standards used in drawing each final map. Each certified final map shall be subject to referendum in the same manner that a statute is subject to referendum pursuant to Section 9 of Article II. The date of certification of a final map to the Secretary of State shall be deemed the enactment date for purposes of Section 9 of Article II.

(j) If the commission does not approve a final map by at least the requisite votes or if voters disapprove a certified final map in a referendum, the Secretary of State shall immediately petition the California Supreme Court for an order directing the appointment of special masters to adjust the boundary lines of that map in accordance with the redistricting criteria and requirements set forth in subdivisions (d), (e), and (f). Upon its approval of the masters' map, the court shall certify the resulting map to the Secretary of State, which map shall constitute the certified final map for the subject type of district.

CALIFORNIA CONSTITUTION ARTICLE 21 REDISTRICTING OF SENATE, ASSEMBLY, CONGRESSIONAL AND BOARD OF EQUAL-IZATION DISTRICTS

SEC. 3. (a) The commission has the sole legal standing to defend any action regarding a certified final map, and shall inform the Legislature if it determines that funds or other resources provided for the operation of the commission are not adequate. The Legislature shall provide adequate funding to defend any action regarding a certified map. The commission has sole authority to determine whether the Attorney General or other legal counsel retained by the commission shall assist in the defense of a certified final map.

(b)

(1) The California Supreme Court has original and exclusive jurisdiction in all proceedings in which a certified final map is challenged or is claimed not to have taken timely effect.

(2) Any registered voter in this state may file a petition for a writ of mandate or writ of prohibition, within 45 days after the commission has certified a final map to the Secretary of State, to bar the Secretary of State from implementing the plan on the grounds that the filed plan violates this Constitution, the United States Constitution, or any federal or state statute.

Any registered voter in this state may also file a petition for a writ of mandate or writ of prohibition to seek relief where a certified final map is subject to a referendum measure that is likely to qualify and stay the timely implementation of the map.

(3) The California Supreme Court shall give priority to ruling on a petition for a writ of mandate or a writ of prohibition filed pursuant to paragraph (2). If the court determines that a final certified map violates this Constitution, the United States Constitution, or any federal or state statute, the court shall fashion the relief that it deems appropriate, including, but not limited to, the relief set forth in subdivision (j) of Section 2. [52]

As you can see, California's approach anticipates and answers many of the logical questions each state must determine for itself.

5. Nonpartisan Blanket Primaries

Another important part of reforming our political process by means of The Democracy Amendments is to have the selection of candidates in the primary elections throughout America be nonpartisan, open, and structured to serve the interests of all citizens, not just the interests of political parties and of only those voters who identify with one political party or another. Therefore, it says in pertinent part:

NONPARTISAN BLANKET PRIMARIES: Section 5. All primary elections in each state for President, Vice-President, Senator and Representative shall be conducted as nonpartisan blanket primaries, including all qualified candidates, regardless of party, with each registered voter entitled to participate, regardless of political party affiliation, using a form of ranked voting so as to result in the selection of two candidates for voters to choose among in the general election.

In a nonpartisan blanket primary, there is no required registration as Democrat or Republican and all candidates, regardless of party, run against each other at once and appear on the same ballot. The two highest voted candidates proceed to the runoff election, regardless of party affiliation

Gone is the closed primary that required voters to be registered with a specific political party in order to vote for partisan candidates. For example, one needed to be a registered Republican to choose among Republican candidates in a closed primary. Registered Democrats similarly could only vote in the Democratic Primary. Independents could usually choose whichever party ballot they want.

Also gone is the party caucus system which several states including Iowa traditionally used, where local gatherings of voters decided which candidates to support and also selected delegates for nominating conventions.

There will no longer be an open primary, which has been used in many states, including my own state of Vermont, where I and other voters are not required to register as belonging to a specific party. Thus I could, for example, vote on either a Republican or a Democratic ballot (but not both) from among those listed on that party's ballot.

The structure of the traditional caucus system and both the open and closed primary systems have created several huge problems. Voter turnout in caucus and primary contests has been traditionally very low, often drawing most heavily from the most committed and passionate voters within any particular party. These small numbers of voters, in turn, end up selecting the candidates that all remaining voters get to choose among in the general election.

For example, in Iowa, a caucus state, in 2012, just 6.5% of the voting eligible population selected the Republican and Democratic candidates to be voted on in the general election[53]. In 2012 in New Hampshire, a primary state, 31.1% participated[54], the highest of any state. The same year in New York, only 1.4% of all eligible voters participated.[55]

Politicians, in order to get elected in the primary, take positions on issues to please this small slice of all voters, and thus our present system tends to elect candidates with more extreme views, whether conservative or liberal, than those held by the majority of American voters. Thus we end up with a Congress less able to collaborate and negotiate to resolve important issues that affect all Americans. We've certainly seen plenty of that lately.

But why does letting small numbers of voters preselect the candidates for the general election best serve the interests of all of us?

It doesn't, and this is precisely why The Democracy Amendments are necessary, as they will allow all registered voters to have an opportunity to participate in selecting the top two primary candidates voters will be able to choose between in the general election.

Washington and California Lead the Way

Recently, Washington State (2008) and California (2010) have begun using a type of nonpartisan blanket primary. All qualified candidates for U.S. Senator or Representative, regardless of party, are included on the same ballot, and allowed to state their party preference. The U.S. Supreme Court upheld the Washington State approach.[56]

With these changes, all voters in both states will begin to play a more effective role in selecting candidates.

The effects of these changes have attracted much attention and discussion and been subsequently evaluated.[57] In both Washington and California, the result for both U.S. Senate and Representative races has been significantly more competition, resulting in more multi-candidate races and more turnover among incumbents.[58]

Will this improvement alone, applied across all states, solve all our representation problems? No! But coupled with other sections of The Democracy Amendments, it is likely to help.

Selecting Between Just Two Primary Winners in the General Election

Both Washington State and California nonpartisan blanket primaries select the top two highest vote getters, regardless of political party, to compete in a run-off against each other in the general election. Regardless of how many primary candidates there are, voters choose the candidate they like best and the two candidates with the highest number of votes then advance to the general election.

One potential danger when there are many primary candidates is that the actual percentage of votes for each candidate can be small. This dynamic encourages "strategic voting," when the candidate you like best isn't one of the candidates likely to win the most votes. If you vote for the candidate that you like the most, you may help elect the candidate you like the least.

Fortunately, there's another solution to this particular problem. It's called "Ranked Choice Voting" or, alternatively, "Instant Runoff Voting." Since both terms speak to the same approach that is sometimes called by one name and sometimes by the other, I'll refer to them as "ranked choice/instant runoff".

The organization FairVote, on their website, has explained the process when electing more than one candidate in a multi-winner election.[59] Below, I've adapted Fair Vote's explanation to apply to selecting our top two primary winners.

Here's how it works. Voters rank candidates in order of their preference. They mark their favorite candidate as first choice, and then indicate their second and additional backup candidates in order of choice. Voters may rank as many candidates as they want, knowing that indicating a later choice candidate will never hurt a more preferred candidate.

To find out who wins, we first need to know how many votes are enough to guarantee victory, which we call the election threshold. That threshold is the number of votes that mathematically guarantees that the candidate cannot lose.

After counting first choices, candidates with more votes than the election threshold are elected. Then, each elected candidate's "surplus," votes are added to the totals of their voters' next choices. For example, if a candidate has 10% more votes than the election threshold, every one of their voters will have 10% of their vote count for their second choice. That way, voters aren't punished for honestly ranking a very popular candidate first.

After the surplus has been counted, the candidate with the fewest votes is eliminated. When a voter's top choice is eliminated, their vote instantly counts for their next choice. That way, voters aren't punished for honestly ranking their favorite candidate first, even if that candidate cannot win.

The process of counting surplus votes and eliminating last-place candidates repeats until the top two primary candidates are selected. This method of counting can be quickly administered using voting machines.

Ranked choice/instant runoff voting to select the top two primary winners maximizes the effectiveness of every vote to ensure that as many voters as possible will help elect a candidate they rank highly. It minimizes wasted votes and the impact of strategic voting, allows voters to have more choices, and encourages positive campaigning and coalition building. It upholds both minority representation and the principle of majority rule.[60]

Other Alternatives

It's important to acknowledge that every system of voting has advantages and disadvantages. Our present system has lots of disadvantages to offset the fact that it's simple and straightforward, even if it often doesn't result in electing a candidate that a majority of us can support.

I hope the voting method we use to select our representatives will be fully and carefully debated as we decide how we should best amend our Constitution to properly serve the interests of citizens.

Fair Vote has selected Ranked Choice/Instant Runoff Voting for the reasons set forth below[61].

Instant Runoff Voting: The Best Method for Single Winner Public Elections

There are many ways of electing officials to single-winner offices other than existing plurality and two-round runoff voting systems. But among these options, we believe instant runoff voting (IRV) offers the most politically practical and common sense option for replacing the faulty plurality voting and two-round runoff systems used in nearly all American elections. The benefits of IRV include:

- Majority rule protected by reducing the "spoiler" dynamic in multi-candidate races
- Both breadth and strength of support needed for candidates to win
- A successful history of implementation
- More positive, issue-oriented campaigns

- Potential taxpayer savings
- Candidates need less money to win

Fair Vote has also evaluated three other alternative voting methods and compared each as to their ability to meet three specific criteria. Fair Vote concludes that each fails to meet the three criteria as well as the ranked choice/instant runoff voting approach. I've quoted from Fair Vote's analysis below.[62]

Evaluating Alternatives to IRV

We evaluate other single-winner election methods on these standards, but initially through three criteria that we see as essential in measuring a method's political viability in the United States:

- Does the method violate the most basic principle of majority rule? In an election with two candidates, we believe the candidate preferred by a majority should always win.

- Does the method require the winner to have core support? We believe a winner should be at least one voter's first choice, meaning they would receive more than 0% in current rules.

- Does the method promote insincere voting? Voters should be likely to vote sincerely, according to the method's rules, and not lose out to tactical voters who vote insincerely.

Alternative 1: Range Voting

With range voting, voters score each candidate: for

example, they could award between 0 and 99 points to each candidate. The candidate with the most points wins. As of early 2007, range voting has not been used in any public election in the world and by very few, if any, private associations.

Bottom-line: Range voting violates all three of our common sense principles of preserving majority rule, requiring a minimum level of core support and rewarding sincere voters.

Example: Consider a range voting election in which 100 voters have the power to assign a score between zero and 99. There are two mediocre candidates. Of the 100 voters, 98 greatly dislike Candidate B, but decide to express their distaste for both candidates by giving one point to Candidate A and none to Candidate B. The remaining two voters prefer Candidate B and are more tactical. They award 99 points to Candidate B and 0 points to Candidate A. The election ends with B beating A by a landslide of 198 to 98 despite the fact that fully 98% of voters preferred Candidate A.

Explanation: This example illustrates how a tactical fringe can overrule a vast majority of voters when the majority votes sincerely and the minority votes tactically. Tactical calculations rise exponentially with the entry of more candidates, at which point winners also do not need to have been any voter's first choice.

Alternative 2: Approval Voting

Approval voting is a form of range voting, with voters limited to awarding candidates a one or zero. As of early 2007, it has not been used in a public election in the United States. The largest association to use it, the Institute of Electrical and Electronic Engineers, abandoned it in 2002 after most voters started to simply cast plurality voting-type ballots.

Bottom-line: *Approval voting violates all three of our common sense principles of preserving majority rule, requiring a minimum level of core support and rewarding sincere voters.*

Example: To illustrate how approval voting violates majority rule, consider a primary with 100 voters and two candidates liked by all voters. 99 voters choose to approve of both candidates even though slightly preferring the first candidate to the second. The 100th voter is a tactical voter and chooses to support only the second candidate. As a result, the second candidate wins by one vote, even though 99% of voters prefer the first candidate.

Explanation: This example shows how voting sincerely in an approval voting election will count against your first choice — e.g., if you approve of a lesser choice, you are giving that candidate support equal to your first choice, and that support could cause your first choice to lose. Voters must always be aware of which candidates might win, and candidates have every incentive to ask supporters privately to vote only for them while publicly pretending otherwise. Many voters will bullet vote (e.g., cast one vote for their first choice and no votes for anyone else), thereby reducing even further voters' ability to express their range of views about candidates. In a three-candidate race, a candidate also can win despite not being even a single voter's first choice.

Alternative 3: Condorcet-Type Rules

Condorcet-type voting rules are ones where voters rank candidates in order of choice, and each candidate is compared with every other in terms of how many voters rank one ahead of the other. If there is a candidate who beats all others in these comparisons he or she is the winner. Condorcet-type voting rules have not been used in any public election in the world as of early 2007, but are used to elect the leadership of some private associations.'

Bottom-line: Condorcet-type voting violates the principle of requiring a minimum level of core support by permitting a candidate to win who would not win a single vote in a plurality election.

Problem 1: With these rules, a candidate can win without being a single voter's first choice. By putting such heavy emphasis on breadth of support, Condorcet-type systems, like approval voting, encourage candidates to be seen as the "least offensive" candidate rather than leaders who take strong positions that might alienate some voters.'

Problem 2: Condorcet comparisons can yield a situation where, in an election among Candidates A,

B and C, Candidate A is preferred to B, B preferred to C, and C preferred to A. In this situation, there is no winner, and a "fallback" method must break the cycle. When this fallback is needed, sincere voters can be punished. Finally, Condorcet-type rules are difficult to count by hand in big elections. Hand-counting is important if problems emerge with voting machines or software.

Scholarly Assessment of IRV

Advocates of range voting, approval voting and Condorcet voting sometimes criticize instant run-off voting for (1) being "non-monotonic" (theoretical situations exist in which improving the ranking of a particular candidate can hurt that candidate's chance of winning because it can change the order of which candidates lose for being in last place) and (2) not always electing the Condorcet winner."

IRV advocates dismiss these criticisms. Potential non-monotonicity with IRV is irrelevant in practice and will not affect voter strategy. We also believe that there are times when the Condorcet winner should not win if that candidate is so lacking in core support that he or she would never win even one vote in a plurality or runoff system. To us, being able to lead and represent people effectively makes it important that a significant number of voters rank the ultimate winner as their first choice."[63]

For all of the above reasons, ranked choice voting has been selected for inclusion in *The Democracy Amendments*.

6. Majority Voting

Also important to The Democracy Amendments is having the winner of the general election enjoy the support of at least half, a majority, of all voters casting ballots. Thus the following:

> **MAJORITY VOTING: Section 6.** *All general elections for President, Vice President and each U.S. Senator and U.S. Representative shall be conducted so that each winner shall only be elected by a majority of more than half of all the votes cast by registered voters.*

With a non-partisan blanket primary having narrowed the candidate choices to the two top primary candidates, it's then relatively easy to have a robust and fully transparent process of debates, interviews, and in depth voter consideration of the merits, or demerits, of the two final contenders.

This amendment would eliminate the current selection of our President and Vice President by the Electoral College as currently set forth in Article II of our U.S. Constitution.

One might argue that if some voters select none of the above, or elect to write in another candidate, it is theoretically possible to have neither of the two candidates elected with a majority of the vote. But this problem is easily solved, by using ranked choice voting as in the primary, to ensure that a winner with majority backing is achieved.

With the approach outlined above, we will have elected our next political leader/representative with a majority of the votes cast. This further provides more unity, and greater ability to lead for those we select. It's also more consistent with the way our country has historically used a winner-take-all system.

However, it's important to acknowledge that a winner-take-all system makes it harder to provide equality of representation for racial minorities and minor parties. For this reason, many other countries use some system of proportional representation where legislators are elected in multi-member districts instead of the single member districts we typically use in America. In these countries, the number of seats that a party, or a person, wins in an election is proportional to the amount of support among voters.[64]

This is an important point, and one I hope will be carefully and fully debated in deciding how we should best amend our Constitution to properly serve the interests of citizens.

7. Use of Public Airwaves and Digital Networks

It's important to remember that we the people control the allocation of our public airwaves and digital networks, through our Federal Communications Commission.

Therefore, another of The Democracy Amendments will have the public airwaves and digital networks actually work to better serve all citizens during the political campaign process, rather than to primarily serve the financial interests of broadcasters. Thus we have:

> **USE OF PUBLIC AIRWAVES AND DIGITAL NETWORKS: Section 7.** *All elections for President, Vice President and all Senators and Representatives shall be conducted with the benefit of free use of the public airways and public digital networks for the purposes of moderated public debates, in-depth interviews with candidates, equal candidate presentations about their background, positions on issues and fitness for elected office, and coverage of the election process shall occur in a manner that provides ample and sufficient opportunity to inform and benefit all potential voters.*

By having the federal Citizen's Election Commission constitutionally mandated to structure the election process to best serve all citizens, we can reach this objective.

In the past, for example, in our recent 2016 presidential primary election, both the Democratic and Republican parties cut deals to have different broadcast networks each host a debate or debates. For our general election, the Commission on Presidential Debates, which is a nonprofit corporation controlled by the Democratic and Republican parties, has run each of the presidential debates held since 1988.[65]

Now, on behalf of all citizens, debates can be set up and moderated independently in accordance with standards set up by the federal Citizens Election Commission, and required to be broadcast broadly at the same time by all broadcasters using the public airways and digital networks. This approach will dramatically increase the number of citizens able to learn about their choice of candidates. Democracy relies on an informed electorate, and the federal Citizens Election Commission will now be constitutionally mandated to take all reasonable steps to make this a reality.

The primary objection to this will come from the media itself. Broadcasters currently make huge profits from political campaign advertising during a prolonged campaign cycle. They will argue that, if, as part of their obligation to have use of our public airways and digital networks, they must now devote a substantial amount of free prime time to further our nation's political process, broadcasters will have to either lose substantial revenue or raise rates among their remaining advertisers.

The answer to this argument is: Yes, that's exactly right, and it's important for our democracy that it is structured so. Broadcasters will need to raise their rates for remaining advertisers if they wish to preserve their profitability.

Under our present system, politicians often use large amounts of negative media advertising about their opponents. Without sufficient resources, an opponent is sometimes unable to effectively respond. With much greater and equal access to the public airways and digital networks, candidates are placed on a much more equal footing. If one candidate wants to make negative comments about an opponent, the opponent can then respond directly in debate, rather than thru an ad campaign in response. With more back and forth between candidates, we're likely to receive a much better and more comprehensive presentation of the facts.

Also under our present system, candidates who are not well known must begin very early in the campaign cycle to get themselves and their positions known and understood by voters. If they are wealthy, or have received large campaign donations, they can spend this money to reach more American voters and get, or keep, an advantage over other candidates. With the enactment of The Democracy Amendments, each viable candidate will have a much more equal opportunity to present their views to voters. Now less well-known candidates who have strong initial backing from those citizens who do know of them and their views, will not find themselves shut off from the opportunity for much more widely broadcast debates and interviews. Large numbers of other Americans will be able to learn about each candidate, and decide for themselves if they like them, or not. It will be a much fairer process for both candidates and citizens.

8. Shorter Election Cycles

With dramatically improved use of our public airways and digital networks constitutionally mandated, we can finally, dramatically shorten our election cycles as follows:

SHORTER ELECTION CYCLES: Section 8. *All elections for President, Vice-President, and all Senators and Representatives shall begin and end within a period of no more than twelve, consecutive months.*

What a wonderful result to finally achieve! Candidates get a much fairer process to have citizens get to know them and their views. Citizens get a fairer process to help them choose whom to support, with ample opportunity to learn about each candidate, their personal and professional backgrounds, their positions on issues, and their ability to articulate and defend those positions in debates. And we all get to use the extra time we gain outside of the shorter election cycle for whatever we want.

Many other nations already do this. It's time for the United States of America to catch up.

9. Full Disclosure

You'd think that it should, and would, be routine to have full and timely disclosure of all campaign funding and expenditures. But you'd be wrong. Politicians now set up the disclosure rules and we presently have, at best, a spotty patchwork.

In this digital age, it's easy enough to set up a real time reporting mechanism for both candidates and independent groups. Moreover it's time to do so, for the benefit of an informed electorate. Thus The Democracy Amendments requires:

> **FULL DISCLOSURE: Section 9.** *All campaign funding and expenditures related to all candidates for President, Vice President and all Senators and Representatives shall be promptly and publically disclosed in a timely manner that shall benefit all registered voters in making their decisions among the candidates prior to the election.*

Citizens Election Commissions will now enforce this mandate. We citizens deserve to know how candidates, and the elections themselves, are being funded, as well as how the money is being spent. Disclosure laws can help to prevent corruption, and the appearance of corruption. They can provide valuable information to voters. Disclosure laws also help enforce other campaign finance laws. For example, if we're worried about the influence of foreign money in elections, disclosure laws tell us how much is coming in.

Often, understanding how the money is being raised and spent provides us with important information about those who might be gaining the most influence, and about the integrity of candidates themselves.

There's a tension between the advantages of disclosure and the privacy of those who feel they may be disadvantaged or harassed if their donations are made public. This amendment makes clear that the advantages of disclosure to the integrity of our democratic process should be the higher priority.

10. Encouraging Voting and Reducing Fraud and Mistakes

Perhaps the most important concept underlying The Democracy Amendments is to have our political system organized and implemented for the overall benefit of all citizens, rather than by and for the primary benefit of any particular political party and its candidates. For this to happen, there must first be an appropriate constitutional mandate for this purpose, created and properly adopted by citizens, plus an entity created for the express purpose of implementing that constitutional mandate on behalf of all citizens regardless of where we live in our United States of America.

Therefore the vehicle to implement The Democracy Amendments is:

*ENCOURAGING VOTING AND REDUCING FRAUD AND MISTAKES: **Section 10.** The Federal Citizens Election Commission shall, in a manner that is open and transparent and independent from legislative and political party influence, establish uniform times, standards and procedures for holding and conducting federal elections in the several states, and also regulate and enforce the campaign behavior and financing of all federal elections for President, Senators and Representatives so as to equally empower voters, encourage maximum voter turnout, prevent fraud, and prevent any regional or local advantage over election outcomes. Each State Citizen Election Commission shall regulate the times, places and* *manner of holding elections in their state in a manner that is consistent with U.S. Constitutional and Statute law as well as standards and procedures set by the Federal Citizens Election Commission.*

The makeup of the Federal Citizens Election Commission, and each state's Citizens Election Commission, is critical if it is to properly represent the interests of all citizens. For this reason, it was covered very carefully in the earlier Section 2, Part IV of part of The Democracy Amendments.

Some will argue that having an overall Federal Citizens Election Commission is usurping the right of each state to set up its own procedures. But if we want a consistent set of laws, regulations and policies working to enhance the rights of all citizens, across state lines, we need both the constitutional mandate of The Democracy Amendments plus the Federal Citizens Election Commission to provide guidance and guidelines in order to properly implement it.

To encourage voting and reduce fraud and mistakes, there are many actions the Federal Citizens Election Commission should take and/or oversee. Here are just a few.

Citizen Financed Elections — As discussed in Section 3 of The Democracy Amendments, providing voters with a small, fixed amount of monetary value to distribute as each voter wishes among candidates will provide a powerful, positive, incentive to vote. While Australia encourages voting by means of a small fine for those who don't vote, the positive incentive of having money to allocate should encourage voters to better learn about candidates, and increase their likelihood to vote.

Improved Voter Perception of the Integrity of our Political System — Recent polls clearly demonstrate citizen's concern about the functioning of our federal political system, but also that citizens are highly skeptical about making any real progress toward fixing it.[66] Having The Democracy Amendments enacted in a manner more under voter control through Article V of our Constitution as discussed in the Introduction of this book, is clearly likely to increase voter confidence in the integrity of our political process. This, in turn, should increase voter turnout.

Uniform Ballot Requirements — Providing uniform requirements for all states with regard to ballot design should help eliminate such problems as the now famous "hanging chads" problem in the 2000 United States presidential election in Florida. As explained in Wikipedia, many voters there used Votomatic-style punched card ballots where incompletely punched holes resulted in partially punched chads. These could be either a "hanging chad", where one or more corners were still attached, or a "fat chad" or "pregnant chad" where all corners were still attached, but an indentation appears to have been made. These votes were not counted by the tabulating machines.[67]

Uniform Requirements for Voting Access — Voter suppression efforts in the United States are discussed in detail on Wikipedia along with comments that are critical to certain aspects of the discussion.[68] Providing uniform requirements for all states with regard to allowing citizens to vote in accordance with constitutional requirements should result in more people being allowed to vote.

11. Enforcement

To ensure The Democracy Amendments are properly enforced, both at the federal level and also within each of the states, and that state action is properly taken within the overall framework of The Democracy Amendments, the following section is included.

> **ENFORCEMENT: Section 11.** *The Congress and the several States shall have concurrent power to implement in a timely manner and enforce the provisions of this article by appropriate legislation, provided that the States shall not abridge uniform federal standards set to enhance the integrity and fairness of the election process on behalf of all voters.*

Any differences of opinion between the federal government and any of the states as to how to properly implement The Democracy Amendments would be resolved by our federal court system. Within each state, questions relating to actions to be determined solely by each state would be resolved by the court system of that state.

12. Operability

Lastly, every amendment to our Constitution must be properly presented and adopted as required by Article V — which controls Amendments to it. The following Section completes this requirement.

> **OPERABILITY: Section 12.** *This article shall be inoperative unless it shall have been ratified as an amendment to the Constitution by the legislatures of three fourths of the several states, or by conventions in the several States, as provided by Article V in the Constitution.*

Although not constitutionally required, many of our initial 27 amendments have added a clause as part of their operability that required adoption by three fourths of the several states within 7 years from being properly introduced. Since the changes proposed by these Democracy Amendments are so important, and have so many parts that need to be thoroughly considered, no particular number of years is required for its adoption.

PART IV

How You Can Help in Your State

A. Considerations for Everyone

We're All Affected, Regardless of Ideology

Whether you are progressive, liberal, moderate, conservative, libertarian, or simply one who doesn't relate to these labels, we are all affected by the dysfunction of our current political system. We all pay, in many ways, both as described in the examples earlier in this book, and in many, many more ways that I didn't describe.

We all pay, whether it's out of our pocket for higher than needed pharmaceutical prices; or in higher taxes to offset revenue that never was collected because Congress chose not to auction off parts of the digital network to broadcasters; or from the loss of large amounts of money from our retirement accounts because both the Democratic and Republican parties chose not to effectively regulate the financial industry in order to remain on good terms with the financial sector, which is a major source of their campaign contributions. This failure was a major contributor to the stock market meltdown beginning in 2007 and 2008.

The above examples, together with many others, cost us far more than what it actually costs to finance our entire federal political process. So it's in our collective interests, regardless of ideology, to fix it so that it prioritizes benefits on behalf of all of us.

Therefore, We All Need to Listen to Each Other's Ideas About How to Best Fix It.

To first succeed in reaching the 34 states needed to call for an Article V Constitutional Convention, as well as to reach the 38 states needed to actually adopt any amendment or amendments that might come from such a convention, proposals need to be acceptable to residents and legislators of both red states and blue states. Thus it's necessary to reach consensus across party and ideological lines about how to best enact reforms.

A good place to seek consensus is to focus on how to best provide our elected federal representatives, as well as federal administrators, with increased incentives to properly represent, legislate, govern, and administrate in the broad public interests of all citizens. And to accomplish this, we need to improve how we can conduct and finance our elections in a manner that prioritizes the interests of citizens above the narrower interests of candidates, political parties, and special interests.

B. As a Legislator or As a Citizen

- You can take many actions that would likely help.

- Initiate action on your own. Resolving this is the paramount public policy issue of our time. Thus you have every right, as we citizens all have, to simply act as you think best.

- Make the ideas and recommendations in this book available to all legislators.

- Reach out to the legislative leaders of all parties, and encourage them to discuss and debate how to be most effective in bringing about reform.

- Reach out to organizations and media within your state to facilitate broad discussion of the issues and recommendations in this book, together with the ideas of others, provided each is proposing reforms that would benefit all citizens.

- Speak often, in whatever way is most effective, about the importance of reforming the way we govern ourselves.

- As a legislator, introduce and build support for a resolution calling for an Article V Constitutional Convention. A model of such a resolution is included in the Appendix C of this book. As a citizen, encourage your legislators to do the same.

- Good luck, and I wish you success, on behalf of all of us!

Appendix A

Books and Authors that Make the Case for Reform

A large amount has been written, researched, and spoken about to document the resulting perversion of law, regulation, and policy caused by the way campaign money is raised by our Washington politicians. The purpose of this book is not to restate the case.

Instead, I'll direct you to a few of the myriad starting points if you'd like to know more. Each of these books sheds different light on the problem.

Lawrence Lessig

Republic, Lost: The Corruption of Equality and the Steps to End It, Second Edition, 2015, Lawrence Lessig. Twelve, a division of the Hachette Book Group. ISBN 978-0446576444

This book is a good place to start. Lessig is the Roy L. Furman Professor of Law at Harvard Law School, and Director of the Edmond J. Safra Center for Ethics at Harvard University. Lessig also founded Rootstrikers[69], an organization dedicated to mobilizing Americans to focus on this issue of corruption, and in 2016 was a Democratic candidate for President. The Democratic Party prevented millions of Americans from hearing him in the debates.

From the publisher: *In an era when special interests funnel huge amounts of money into our government —*

driven by shifts in campaign-finance rules and brought to new levels by the Supreme Court in Citizens United v. Federal Election Commission — trust in our government has reached an all-time low. More than ever before, Americans believe that money buys results in Congress, and that business interests wield control over our legislature.

With heartfelt urgency and a keen desire for righting wrongs, Harvard law professor Lawrence Lessig takes a clear-eyed look at how we arrived at this crisis: how fundamentally good people, with good intentions, have allowed our democracy to be co-opted by outside interests, and how this exploitation has become entrenched in the system. Rejecting simple labels and reductive logic — and instead using examples that resonate as powerfully on the Right as on the Left — Lessig seeks out the root causes of our situation. He plumbs the issues of campaign financing and corporate lobbying, revealing the human faces and follies that have allowed corruption to take such a foothold in our system. He puts the issues in terms that non-wonks can understand, using real-world analogies and real human stories. And ultimately he calls for widespread mobilization and a new Constitutional Convention, presenting achievable solutions for regaining control of our corrupted-but redeemable-representational system. In this way, Lessig plots a roadmap for returning our republic to its intended greatness.

While America may be divided, Lessig vividly champions the idea that we can succeed if we accept that corruption is our common enemy and that we must find a way to fight against it. In Republic, Lost, he not only makes this need palpable and clear — he gives us the practical and intellectual tools to do something about it.

As originally stated on Rootstrikers[70], an advocacy organization co-founded by Lessig: "Our government is corrupt. Not corrupt in any criminal sense. But corrupt in a perfectly legal sense: special interests bend the levers of power to benefit them at the expense of the rest of us. Both parties are part of the problem. Both have become dependent upon the campaign funding of the tiniest slice of the American people — not to mention the funding of corporations and other non-citizens. That dependency is this corruption.

Only the people can force lasting change on this broken system. That change begins with understanding: The people must recognize that corruption is not just one among many important problems. Corruption is the root problem that makes solving the others so difficult.[71]

Martin Gilens

Affluence and Influence: Economic Inequality and Political Power in America, by Martin Gilens, Princeton University Press, 2012. ISBN 978-0691153971

Gilens is a political science professor at Princeton, and this book is the result of extensive research by Martin and, I assume, with a great deal of assistance from graduate students and others. Fair warning: this book is not an easy read. It presents like the write-up of a major research project, which is exactly what it is, and an advanced degree in statistics would be helpful if one is to understand it in depth. Nevertheless, it's findings and conclusions are both significant and very important. One doesn't need an advanced degree to absorb just how unsettling they are for all of us who are concerned about the effectiveness of our current representative democracy.

From the publisher: *Can a country be a democracy if its government only responds to the preferences of the rich? In an ideal democracy, all citizens should have equal influence on government policy—but as this book demonstrates, America's policymakers respond almost exclusively to the preferences of the economically advantaged. Affluence and Influence definitively explores how political inequality in the United States has evolved over the last several decades and how this growing disparity has been shaped by interest groups, parties, and elections.*

With sharp analysis and an impressive range of data, Martin Gilens looks at thousands of proposed policy changes, and the degree of support for each among poor, middle-class, and affluent Americans. His findings are staggering: when preferences of low- or middle-income Americans diverge from those of the affluent, there is virtually no relationship between policy outcomes and the desires of less advantaged groups. In contrast, affluent Americans' preferences exhibit a substantial relationship with policy outcomes, whether their preferences are shared by lower-income groups or not. Gilens shows that representational inequality is spread widely across different policy domains and time periods. Yet Gilens also shows that under specific circumstances the preferences of the middle class and, to a lesser extent, the poor, do seem to matter. In particular, impending elections — especially presidential elections — and an even partisan division in Congress mitigate representational inequality and boost responsiveness to the preferences of the broader public.

At a time when economic and political inequality in the United States only continues to rise, Affluence and Influence raises important questions about whether

American democracy is truly responding to the needs of all its citizens.

Richard Painter

Taxation Only With Representation, Richard Painter, 2016, Take Back our Republic, ISBN 978-1939324122

Painter is a professor at the University of Minnesota, and former chief ethics lawyer for President George W. Bush.

> From the publisher: *This book is the first comprehensive discussion of corruption in campaign finance from the viewpoint of a political conservative. In this book, Richard Painter discusses how our money driven campaign system undermines the vision of our Founding Fathers and just about every principle that conservatives believe in. Painter then lays out a plan for reform that conservatives, and the Supreme Court, will embrace: defining the government's right to tax its citizens in a way that will give each citizen a real voice in funding campaigns for elected officials.*

Zephyr Teachout

Corruption in America: From Benjamin Franklin's Snuff Box to Citizens United, Zephyr Teachout, Harvard University Press, 2016. ISBN 9780674659988

> From the publisher: *When Louis XVI presented Benjamin Franklin with a snuff box encrusted with diamonds and inset with the King's portrait, the gift troubled Americans: it threatened to "corrupt" Franklin by clouding his judgment or altering his attitude toward the French in subtle psychological ways. This broad understanding of political corruption—rooted in ideals of*

civic virtue—was a driving force at the Constitutional Convention.

For two centuries the framers' ideas about corruption flourished in the courts, even in the absence of clear rules governing voters, civil officers, and elected officials. Should a law that was passed by a state legislature be overturned because half of its members were bribed? What kinds of lobbying activity were corrupt, and what kinds were legal? When does an implicit promise count as bribery? In the 1970s the U.S. Supreme Court began to narrow the definition of corruption, and the meaning has since changed dramatically. No case makes that clearer than Citizens United.

In 2010, one of the most consequential Court decisions in American political history gave wealthy corporations the right to spend unlimited money to influence elections. Justice Anthony Kennedy's majority opinion treated corruption as nothing more than explicit bribery, a narrow conception later echoed by Chief Justice Roberts in deciding McCutcheon v. FEC in 2014. With unlimited spending transforming American politics for the worse, warns Zephyr Teachout, Citizens United and McCutcheon were not just bad law but bad history. If the American experiment in self-government is to have a future, then we must revive the traditional meaning of corruption and embrace an old ideal.

Joseph Stiglitz

The Price of Inequality, by Joseph E. Stiglitz, W.W. Norton & Company, 2013. ISBN 978-0393345063

Stiglitz, a winner of the Nobel Prize in economics, has written a book that looks through an economist's lens at the interaction of market forces and political machinations that underlie the resulting inequality in America today. Stiglitz shows how, over time, our politics has shaped the market in ways that advantage those at the top at the expense of the rest of society.

Mickey Edwards

The Parties Versus the People, by Mickey Edwards, Yale University Press, 2013. ISBN 978-0300198218

Edwards speaks with passion, as a former Republican congressman, about a political system so paralyzed by partisanship it is almost incapable of placing national interest ahead of the blind pursuit of political advantage. Mickey discusses and makes recommendations about several possible improvements.

Thomas Mann and Norman Ornstein

It's Even Worse Than It Looks, Thomas Mann and Norman Ornstein, Basic books, 2016. ISBN: 978-0465096206 Note: this is a new, revised edition.

> From the publisher: *Hyperpartisanship has gridlocked the American government. Congress's approval ratings are at record lows, and both Democrats and Republicans are disgusted by the government's inability to get anything done. In It's Even Worse than It Looks, Congressional scholars Thomas E. Mann and Norman*

J. Ornstein present a grim picture of how party polarization and tribal politics have led Congress—and the United States—to the brink of institutional failure.

In this revised edition, the authors bring their seminal book up-to-date in a political environment that is more divided than ever. The underlying dynamics of the situation—extremist Republicans holding government hostage to their own ideological, anti-government beliefs—have only gotten worse, further bolstering their argument that Republicans are not merely ideologically different from Democrats, but engaged in a unique form of politics that undermines the system itself. Without a fundamental change in the character and course of the Republican Party, we may have a long way to go before we hit rock bottom.

David Cay Johnston

Free Lunch — How the Wealthiest Americans Enrich Themselves at Government Expense (and Stick You with the Bill), David Cay Johnston, Portfolio, 2008. ISBN 978-1591842484

Johnston, provides an in-depth look, with many concrete examples, of today's government policies and spending that reach deep into the wallets of the many for the benefit of the wealthy few.

Hedrick Smith

Who Stole the American Dream, by Hedrick Smith, Random House Trade Paperbacks, 2013. ISBN 978-0812982053

Smith chronicles how, over the past four decades, a series of seismic changes dismantled the American Dream. He reveals how pivotal laws and policies were altered while the public wasn't looking, why moderate politicians got shoved to the sidelines, and how Wall Street wins politically by hiring over 1,400 former government officials as lobbyists.

Derek Cressman

When Money Talks: The High Price of "Free" Speech and Democracy, 1st Edition, by Derek Cressman, Berrett-Koehler Publishers, 2016. ISBN 9781626565760

Cressman began working professionally to reduce big money in politics in 1995 with such nonpartisan organizations as Common Cause and the Public Interest Research Group. As USPIRG's democracy program director, he was the first professional advocate in Washington, DC to support a constitutional amendment to limit campaign spending.

As he explains on his website: "Americans know that the corrupting influence of special interest money is destroying our democratic process. Now they want to know what they can do about it. Derek Cressman gives us the tools, both intellectual and tactical, to fight back."

Robert Sheer

The Great American Stickup: How Reagan Republicans and Clinton Democrats Enriched Wall Street While Mugging Main Street, Robert Sheer, Nation Books, 2010. ISBN 9781568584348

From the publisher: *In* The Great American Stickup, *celebrated journalist Robert Scheer uncovers the hidden story behind one of the greatest financial crimes of our time: the Wall Street financial crash of 2008 and the consequent global recession. Instead of going where other journalists have gone in search of this story—the board rooms and trading floors of the big Wall Street firms — Scheer goes back to Washington, D.C., a ver-itable crime scene, beginning in the 1980s, where the captains of the finance industry, their lobbyists and al-lies among leading politicians destroyed an American regulatory system that had been functioning effectively since the era of the New Deal.*

This is a story largely forgotten or overlooked by the mainstream media, who wasted more than two de-cades with their boosterish coverage of Wall Street. Scheer argues that the roots of the disaster go back to the free-market propaganda of the Reagan years and, most damagingly, to the bipartisan deregulation of the banking industry undertaken with the full support of "progressive" Bill Clinton.

In fact, if this debacle has a name, Scheer suggests, it is the "Clinton Bubble," that era when the administration let its friends on Wall Street write legislation that razed decades of robust financial regulation. It was Wall Street and Democratic Party darling Robert Rubin along with his clique of economist super-friends—Alan Greenspan, Lawrence Summers, and a few others— who inflated a giant real estate bubble by purposely not regulating the derivatives market, resulting in the pain and hardship millions are experiencing now.

The Great American Stickup is both a brilliant tell-ing of the story of the Clinton financial clique and the havoc it wrought—informed by whistleblowers such as Brooksley Born, who goes on the record for Scheer— and an unsparing anatomy of the American business and political class. It is also a cautionary tale: those who form the nucleus of the Clinton clique are now advising the Obama administration.

Jane Mayer

Dark Money, The Hidden History of the Billionaires Behind the Rise of the Radical Right, Jane Mayer, Doubleday, 2016. ISBN 9780385535595

From the publisher: *Why is America living in an age of profound economic inequality? Why, despite the desperate need to address climate change, have even modest environmental efforts been defeated again and again? Why have protections for employees been decimated? Why do hedge-fund billionaires pay a far lower tax rate than middle-class workers?*

The conventional answer is that a popular uprising against "big government" led to the ascendancy of a broad-based conservative movement. But as Jane Mayer shows in this powerful, meticulously reported history, a network of exceedingly wealthy people with extreme libertarian views bankrolled a systematic, step-by-step plan to fundamentally alter the American political system.

The network has brought together some of the richest people on the planet. Their core beliefs—that taxes are a form of tyranny; that government oversight of business is an assault on freedom—are sincerely held. But these beliefs also advance their personal and corporate interests: Many of their companies have run afoul of federal pollution, worker safety, securities, and tax laws.

The chief figures in the network are Charles and David Koch, whose father made his fortune in part by building oil refineries in Stalin's Russia and Hitler's Germany. The patriarch later was a founding member of the John Birch Society, whose politics were so radical it believed Dwight Eisenhower was a communist. The brothers were schooled in a political philosophy that asserted the only role of government is to provide security and to enforce property rights.

When libertarian ideas proved decidedly unpopular with voters, the Koch brothers and their allies chose another path. If they pooled their vast resources, they could fund an interlocking array of organizations that could work in tandem to influence and ultimately control academic institutions, think tanks, the courts, statehouses, Congress, and, they hoped, the presidency. Richard Mellon Scaife, the mercurial heir to banking and oil fortunes, had the brilliant insight that most of their political activities could be written off as tax-deductible "philanthropy."

These organizations were given innocuous names such as Americans for Prosperity. Funding sources were hidden whenever possible. This process reached its apotheosis with the allegedly populist Tea Party movement, abetted mightily by the Citizens United decision—a case conceived of by legal advocates funded by the network.

The political operatives the network employs are disciplined, smart, and at times ruthless. Mayer documents instances in which people affiliated with these groups hired private detectives to impugn whistle-blowers, journalists, and even government investigators. And their efforts have been remarkably successful. Libertarian views on taxes and regulation, once far outside the mainstream and still rejected by most Americans, are ascendant in the majority of state governments, the Supreme Court, and Congress. Meaningful environmental, labor, finance, and tax reforms have been stymied.

Jane Mayer spent five years conducting hundreds of in-terviews-including with several sources within the net-work-and scoured public records, private papers, and court proceedings in reporting this book. In a taut and utterly convincing narrative, she traces the byzantine trail of the billions of dollars spent by the network and provides vivid portraits of the colorful figures behind the new American oligarchy.

Dark Money *is a book that must be read by anyone who cares about the future of American democracy.*

Wendell Potter

Nation on the Take: How Big Money Corrupts Our Democracy and What We Can Do About It, Wendell Potter and Nick Penniman, Bloomsbury Press, 2016. ISBN 9781632861092

From the publisher: *American democracy has become coin operated. Special interest groups increasingly con-trol every level of government. The necessity of raising huge sums of campaign cash has completely changed the character of politics and policy-making, determin-ing what elected representatives stand for and how they spend their time. The marriage of great wealth and in-tense political influence has rendered our country un-able to address our most pressing problems, from run-away government spending to climate change to the wealth gap. It also defines our daily lives: from the cars we drive to the air we breathe to the debt we owe.*

In this powerful work of reportage, Wendell Potter and Nick Penniman, two vigilant watchdogs, expose legal-ized corruption and link it to the kitchen-table issues citizens face every day. Inciting our outrage, the au-thors then inspire us by introducing us to the army of reformers laying the groundwork for change, ready to be called into action. *The battle plan for reform presented is practical, realistic, and concrete. No one-except some lobbyists and major political donors — likes business as usual, and this book intends to help forge a new army of reformers who are compelled by a patriotic duty to fight for a better democracy.*

An impassioned, infuriating, yet ultimately hopeful call to arms, Nation on the Take *lays bare the reach of moneyed interests and charts a way forward, toward the recovery of America's original promise.*

NOTE: *The above books represent only a partial list of those weighing in on the current effectiveness of the way we govern ourselves. But it should provide excellent starting points to anyone wishing to better understand the problem Americans face.*

Appendix B

The Democracy Amendments As Ten Separate Amendments

Proposing an Amendment to the Constitution of the United States in order to: improve the way we elect our representatives; provide Congress with increased incentives to properly represent, legislate and govern in the broad public interests of all citizens; and to conduct and finance our elections, in a manner that prioritizes the broad public interests of citizens above the narrower interests of candidates, political parties, and special interests, so as to enhance the way we the people govern ourselves.

AMENDMENT 28

RIGHT TO VOTE: Section 1. Every citizen of the United States, who is of legal voting age, shall have the fundamental right to vote in any public election held in the jurisdiction in which the citizen resides.

Section 2. The Congress and the several States shall have concurrent power to implement in a timely manner and enforce the provisions of this article by appropriate legislation, provided that the States shall not abridge uniform federal standards set to enhance the integrity and fairness of the election process on behalf of all voters.

Section 3. This article shall be inoperative unless it shall have been ratified as an amendment to the Constitution by the legislatures of three fourths of the several states, or by conventions in the several States, as provided by Article V in the Constitution.

AMENDMENT 29

CITIZEN ELECTION COMMISSIONS: *Section 1. Congress and each State shall establish Citizens Election Commissions to regulate and maintain the integrity and fairness of the election process on behalf of voters, each of which shall have a majority of members who are not current or recent legislators or members of any political party, and all members shall conduct its affairs in order to be independent from legislative and political party influence.*

Section 2. The Congress and the several States shall have concurrent power to implement in a timely manner and enforce the provisions of this article by appropriate legislation, provided that the States shall not abridge uniform federal standards set to enhance the integrity and fairness of the election process on behalf of all voters.

Section 3. This article shall be inoperative unless it shall have been ratified as an amendment to the Constitution by the legislatures of three fourths of the several states, or by conventions in the several States, as provided by Article V in the Constitution.

AMENDMENT 30

CITIZEN FINANCING: *Section 1. All federal elections for Senator, Representative, President and Vice President, shall be publicly financed in a manner that, in ma-*

jor part, provides each registered voter in each primary and general election with an equal amount of monetary value from the federal treasury to be allocated among the primary and general election candidates as each registered voter sees fit.

Section 2. *The Congress and the several States shall have concurrent power to implement in a timely manner and enforce the provisions of this article by appropriate legislation, provided that the States shall not abridge uniform federal standards set to enhance the integrity and fairness of the election process on behalf of all voters.*

Section 3. *This article shall be inoperative unless it shall have been ratified as an amendment to the Constitution by the legislatures of three fourths of the several states, or by conventions in the several States, as provided by Article V in the Constitution.*

AMENDMENT 31

CITIZEN REDISTRICTING: Section 1. *Each State's Citizen Election Commission shall conduct the periodic redrawing of voting district lines in an open and transparent process so as to produce districts that comply with U.S. Constitutional and Statute law and are independent from legislative and political party influence.*

Section 2. *The Congress and the several States shall have concurrent power to implement in a timely manner and enforce the provisions of this article by appropriate legislation, provided that the States shall not abridge uniform federal standards set to enhance the integrity and fairness of the election process on behalf of all voters.*

Section 3. *This article shall be inoperative unless it shall have been ratified as an amendment to the Constitution by the legislatures of three fourths of the several states, or by conventions in the several States, as provided by Article V in the Constitution.*

AMENDMENT 32

NONPARTISAN BLANKET PRIMARIES: Section 1. *All primary elections in each state for President, Vice-President, Senator and Representative shall be conducted as nonpartisan blanket primaries, including all qualified candidates, regardless of party, with each registered voter entitled to participate, regardless of political party affiliation, using a form of ranked voting so as to result in the selection of two candidates for voters to choose among in the general election.*

Section 2. *The Congress and the several States shall have concurrent power to implement in a timely manner and enforce the provisions of this article by appropriate legislation, provided that the States shall not abridge uniform federal standards set to enhance the integrity and fairness of the election process on behalf of all voters.*

Section 3. *This article shall be inoperative unless it shall have been ratified as an amendment to the Constitution by the legislatures of three fourths of the several states, or by conventions in the several States, as provided by Article V in the Constitution.*

AMENDMENT 33

MAJORITY VOTING: Section 1. All general elections for President, Vice President and each U.S. Senator and U.S. Representative shall be conducted so that each winner shall only be elected by a majority of more than half of all the votes cast by registered voters.

Section 2. The Congress and the several States shall have concurrent power to implement in a timely manner and enforce the provisions of this article by appropriate legislation, provided that the States shall not abridge uniform federal standards set to enhance the integrity and fairness of the election process on behalf of all voters.

Section 3. This article shall be inoperative unless it shall have been ratified as an amendment to the Constitution by the legislatures of three fourths of the several states, or by conventions in the several States, as provided by Article V in the Constitution.

AMENDMENT 34

USE OF PUBLIC AIRWAVES AND DIGITAL NETWORKS: Section 1. All elections for President, Vice President and all Senators and Representatives shall be conducted with the benefit of free use of the public airways and public digital networks for the purposes of moderated public debates, in-depth interviews with candidates, equal candidate presentations about their background, positions on issues and fitness for elected office, and coverage of the election process shall occur in a manner that provides ample and sufficient opportunity to inform and benefit all potential voters.

Section 2. *The Congress and the several States shall have concurrent power to implement in a timely manner and enforce the provisions of this article by appropriate legislation, provided that the States shall not abridge uniform federal standards set to enhance the integrity and fairness of the election process on behalf of all voters.*

Section 3. *This article shall be inoperative unless it shall have been ratified as an amendment to the Constitution by the legislatures of three fourths of the several states, or by conventions in the several States, as provided by Article V in the Constitution.*

AMENDMENT 35

SHORTER ELECTION CYCLES: Section 1. *All elections for President, Vice-President, and all Senators and Representatives shall begin and end within a period of no more than twelve, consecutive months.*

Section 2. *The Congress and the several States shall have concurrent power to implement in a timely manner and enforce the provisions of this article by appropriate legislation, provided that the States shall not abridge uniform federal standards set to enhance the integrity and fairness of the election process on behalf of all voters.*

Section 3. *This article shall be inoperative unless it shall have been ratified as an amendment to the Constitution by the legislatures of three fourths of the several states, or by conventions in the several States, as provided by Article V in the Constitution.*

AMENDMENT 36

FULL DISCLOSURE: Section 1. All campaign funding and expenditures related to all candidates for President, Vice President and all Senators and Representatives shall be promptly and publically disclosed in a timely manner that shall benefit all registered voters in making their decisions among the candidates prior to the election.

Section 2. The Congress and the several States shall have concurrent power to implement in a timely manner and enforce the provisions of this article by appropriate legislation, provided that the States shall not abridge uniform federal standards set to enhance the integrity and fairness of the election process on behalf of all voters.

Section 3. This article shall be inoperative unless it shall have been ratified as an amendment to the Constitution by the legislatures of three fourths of the several states, or by conventions in the several States, as provided by Article V in the Constitution.

AMENDMENT 37

ENCOURAGING VOTING AND REDUCING FRAUD AND MISTAKES: Section 1. The Federal Citizens Election Commission shall, in a manner that is open and transparent and independent from legislative and political party influence, establish uniform times, standards and procedures for holding and conducting federal elections in the several states, and also regulate and enforce the campaign behavior and financing of all federal elections for President, Senators and Representatives so as to equally empower voters, encourage maximum voter turnout, prevent fraud, and prevent any re-

gional or local advantage over election outcomes. Each State Citizen Election Commission shall regulate the times, places and manner of holding elections in their state in a manner that is consistent with U.S. Constitutional and Statute law as well as standards and procedures set by the Federal Citizens Election Commission.

Section 2. The Congress and the several States shall have concurrent power to implement in a timely manner and enforce the provisions of this article by appropriate legislation, provided that the States shall not abridge uniform federal standards set to enhance the integrity and fairness of the election process on behalf of all voters.

Section 3. This article shall be inoperative unless it shall have been ratified as an amendment to the Constitution by the legislatures of three fourths of the several states, or by conventions in the several States, as provided by Article V in the Constitution.

Appendix C

A Model Resolution For States

A RESOLUTION from the state of (your state) to make application to the Congress of the United States to call an Article V convention in order to propose an amendment, or amendments, to the Constitution of the United States, for submission to the states for ratification. The amendment or amendments shall be limited in purpose, to improve the way we elect our representatives; provide Congress with increased incentives to properly represent, legislate and govern in the broad public interests of all citizens; and to conduct and finance our elections, in a manner that prioritizes the broad public interests of citizens above the narrower interests of candidates, political parties, and special interests, so as to enhance the way we the people govern ourselves

WHEREAS, As our Declaration of Independence declared in 1776: "We hold these truths to be self-evident, that all men are created equal, that they are endowed by their Creator with certain unalienable Rights, — that among these are Life, Liberty and the pursuit of Happiness, — That to secure these rights, Governments are instituted among Men, deriving their just powers from the consent of the governed, — That whenever any Form of Government becomes destructive of these ends, it is the Right of the People to alter or abolish it, ..." and

WHEREAS, we do not seek to abolish our Government, but we do seek to alter and improve it for the purposes stated above, and

WHEREAS, there is voluminous evidence documenting the fact that the way we currently select our candidates, conduct and finance our elections, and subsequently enact laws, regulations, and policies, frequently prioritizes the narrower interests of candidates, political parties, and special interests above the broad public interests of citizens, now therefore be it

RESOLVED, that the people of the State of [your state], speaking through its legislature, and pursuant to Article V of the United States Constitution, hereby make application to the Congress of the United States to call an Article V convention, as soon as two-thirds of the several States have applied for a convention, to propose an amendment, or amendments, to the Constitution of the United States, for submission to the states for ratification. The amendment or amendments, shall be limited in purpose, to provide Congress with increased incentives to properly represent, legislate, and govern in the broad public interests of all citizens, and to conduct and finance our elections, in a manner that prioritizes the broad public interests of citizens above the narrower interests of candidates, political parties, and special interests, so as to improve the way we the people govern ourselves; and they shall all be in general accordance with the attached Democracy Amendment, and be it

FURTHER RESOLVED, that the total number of State of [your state] delegates to said convention shall be determined by the legislature, and shall be comprised of two equal parts. One half shall be selected by the legisla-

ture, and consist of individuals currently elected to state and local office, and the other half shall be selected by election, in each Congressional district for the purpose of serving as delegates. All individuals elected or appointed to federal office, now or in the past, are prohibited from serving as delegates to the convention. This state retains the ability to restrict or expand the power of its delegates within the limits expressed above; and be it

FURTHER RESOLVED, that this application by this legislature constitutes a continuing application in accordance with Article V of the Constitution of the United States until at least two-thirds of the Legislatures of the several states have made application for a similar convention pursuant to Article V and said convention is convened by Congress; and be it

FURTHER RESOLVED, that the Secretary of State of the state of [your state] transmit copies of this resolution to the President of the United States; the Vice President of the United States in his capacity as presiding officer of the United States Senate, the Speaker of the United States House of Representatives, the Minority Leader of the United States House of Representatives, the President Pro Tempore of the United States Senate, and to each Senator and Representative from [your state] in the Congress of the United States, together with the respectful request that the full and complete text of this resolution be printed in the Congressional Record, and that copies also be sent to the presiding officers of each legislative body of each of the several States, requesting the cooperation of the States in issuing an application compelling Congress to call a convention for proposing amendments pursuant to Article V of the U.S. Constitution.

Afterward

This book reflects my evolving understanding of, and deep concern for, revising our U.S. Constitution to vastly improve both the way we choose those we elect to represent us, and the way they actually do represent us once elected.

Amending and improving our Constitution is a difficult and daunting task. Accomplishing it requires large percentages of our population, of all ideologies, to reach consensus on the best approach.

I'm grateful to be among the ever-increasing number of American citizens working to accomplish this goal. It's important work. Thanks to everyone else involved (you know who you are) for all your past and continuing efforts.

I've drawn inspiration and increased understanding from many of those mentioned in this book. Thank you!

After writing this book, it needed to be properly designed and made ready for publishing. I'm very thankful to have had "my good shepherd" Kitty Werner provide expert technical assistance, plus great advice, with all aspects of that process.

Special thanks go to my life partner, Sally Howe, who has supported my work in countless ways. Her editing skill has made this a better book.

End Notes

1   In possession of the author, as provided by Dennis Burke, supporter and speech-writer for GrannyD, and also subsequent author of books about her advocacy and life. Also available online at: http://www.spectacle.org/0600/granny.html.

2   Ibid.

3   In possession of the author as written by the Honorable Phil Hoff, Vermont's former Governor.

4   Lawrence Lessig, 2016 Edition of *Republic Lost, The Corruption of Equality and the Steps to End It.*

5   THE RECORDS OF THE FEDERAL CONVENTION OF 1787, 2, note 5, at 629; See also: Harvard Journal of Law & Public Policy, NOTE — THE OTHER WAY TO AMEND THE CONSTITUTION: THE ARTICLE V CONSTITUTIONAL CONVENTION AMENDMENT PROCESS, II. HISTORY A. The Constitutional Convention, p. 1007.

6   Fair Vote, Right to Vote Initiative, "Why We Need a Right to Vote Amendment — State authority over voting creates unnecessary voting difficulties" available at link: http://www.fairvote.org/right_to_vote_amendment - why_we_need_a_right_to_vote_amendment.

7   Fair Vote, available at link: http://www.fairvote.org

8   Ibid., Right to Vote Amendment, available at link: http://www.fairvote.org/right_to_vote_amendment - why_we_need_a_right_to_vote_amendment.

9   Ibid., available at link: http://www.fairvote.org/right_to_vote_amendment#the_bill_house_joint_resolution_25.

10   Ibid., Why We Need a Right to Vote Amendment, available at link: http://www.fairvote.org/right_to_vote_amendment#why_we_

need_a_right_to_vote_amendment.

11   Ibid., Right to Vote FAQ, "I've never had a problem voting. Don't we already have a right to vote?", available at link: http://www.fairvote.org/right_to_vote_amendment#right_to_vote_faq

12   Ibid., Right to Vote FAQ, "I've never had a problem voting. Don't we already have a right to vote?", available at link: http://www.fairvote.org/right_to_vote_amendment#right_to_vote_faq

13   Ibid., Right to Vote FAQ, "I've never had a problem voting. Don't we already have a right to vote?", available at link: http://www.fairvote.org/right_to_vote_amendment#right_to_vote_faq

14   Ibid., Right to Vote FAQ, "Is the right to vote a partisan issue?", available at link: http://www.fairvote.org/right_to_vote_amendment#right_to_vote_faq

15   Ibid., Right to Vote FAQ, "Don't citizens have a right to vote in presidential elections?", available at link: http://www.fairvote.org/right_to_vote_amendment#right_to_vote_faq

16   California Citizens Redistricting Commission, "FAQ", available at link: http://wedrawthelines.ca.gov/faq.html

17   Lawrence Lessig, Republic Lost, The Corruption of Equality and the Steps to End It, 2016 Edition, published by Hachette Book Group, Page 15, based upon information provided him by OpenSecrets.org.

18   Martin Gilens, Economic Inequality and Political Power in America, Princeton University Press, Page 81.

19   Written statement by Phil Hoff, Vermont's former governor, in the author's possession.

20   James Madison, The Federalist Papers, No. 57.

21   Lawrence Lessig, as expressed at "Mission" on his campaign website, available at https://lessig2016.us.

22   2016 Presidential Hopefuls Sorted by FEC Total Receipts, as of 10/22/2015, available at http://www.thegreenpapers.com/P16/candidates.phtml?sort=f.

23   Ibid.

24   Ibid.

25   Ibid.

26   Voter Registration Statistics, on the website of Voting Statistics/ Statistical Brain, as presented on January18th, 2016 at the following link: http://www.statisticbrain.com/voting-statistics/.

27   Ibid.

28   Lawrence Lessig, in several blog and press releases within "News & Updates" on his campaign website, available at: https:// lessig2016.us.

29   Buddy Roemer Presidential Campaign, 2012, Candidate Campaign Participation, available at: https://en.wikipedia.org/wiki/Buddy_Roemer_presidential_campaign,_2012

30   Ibid.

31   Ibid.

32   Ibid.

33   Biography.com, Boss Tweed biography, available at: http://www.biography.com/people/boss-tweed-20967991

34   Ibid.

35   Federal Election Commission, How do I register as a candidate for federal office, available at: http://www.fec.gov/ans/answers_candidate.shtml

36   Constitution of the United States of America, Article II, Section. 1.

37   Center for Responsive Politics, The 2012 Election: Our Price Tag (Finally) for the Whole Ball of Wax, available at: http://www.opensecrets.org/news/2013/03/the-2012-election-our-price-tag-fin/

38   Voter Registration Statistics, on the website of Voting Statistics/ Statistical Brain, as presented on January18th, 2016 at the following link: http://www.statisticbrain.com/voting-statistics/

39   Wikipedia, 2016 United States Federal Budget, available at: https://en.wikipedia.org/wiki/2016_United_States_federal_budget and Fiscal Year 2016 Budget of the U.S. Government, available at: https://www.gpo.gov/fdsys/pkg/BUDGET-2016-BUD/pdf/BUDGET-2016-BUD.pdf

40   For the 2011–2012 two-year election cycle the total cost was about $6.3 billion, divided by 2 years equals about $3.15 billion per year. Center for Responsive Politics, The 2012 Election: Our Price Tag (Finally) for the Whole Ball of Wax, available at: http://www.

opensecrets.org/news/2013/03/the-2012-election-our-price-tag-fin/

41    $4 billion dollars divided by the total U.S. Population of 322,876,322 equals $12.39 per person as of January 23, 2016 on the U.S. Census *U.S.* (and World) Population Clock for U.S. Population, available at: http://www.census.gov/popclock/

42   Total Cost of the Federal Election in 2015/2016 (Est) is $8,000,000,000. Divide this by 2 for an Annualized Cost of $4,000,000,000. Divide this $4 billion by the Total Number of U.S. Households in the 2010 Census which is: 12,611,029. This will give you the Annual Election Cost per Household (annual cost/households) which is $35.52

43   Robert W. McChesney, *The Nation Digital Edition, Digital Highway Robbery,* available at: http://www.radiodiversity.com/hiwayrobbery.html

44   Valerie Paris, OECD, *Why do Americans spend so much on pharmaceuticals,* PBS Newshour, February 7, 2014, available at: http://www.pbs.org/newshour/updates/americans-spend-much-pharmaceuticals/

45   Statista — *The Statistics Portal, Statistics and facts about the Pharmaceutical Industry in the U.S.,* available at: http://www.statista.com/topics/1719/pharmaceutical-industry/

46   Open Secrets.org, Center for Responsive Politics, Influence & Lobbying, Finance /Insurance/Real Estate, available at: https://www.opensecrets.org/industries/indus.php?Ind=F

47   Ibid.

48   Wikipedia, *"Carried Interest, Taxation, United States",* available at: https://en.wikipedia.org/wiki/Carried_interest

49   American household net worth fell from a pre-recession peak of $68 trillion in Q3 2007 to $55 trillion by Q1 2009, FRED Database-Household Net Worth-Retrieved October 2015, available at: https://research.stlouisfed.org/fred2/series/TNWBSHNO

50    $13 Trillion divided by 112,611,029 U.S. households in per the 2010 Census equals a loss of approximately $115,443 per household.

51   FRED Database—Unemployment Rate—Retrieved October 2015, available at: https://research.stlouisfed.org/fred2/series/UN-RATE

52   California Constitution Article 21.

53   United States Elections Project, "2012 Presidential Nomination Contest Turnout Rates," available at: http://www.electproject.org/2012p

54   Ibid.

55   Ibid.

56   On March 18, 2008, the United States Supreme Court ruled in Washington State Grange v. Washington State Republican Party that Washington's Initiative 872 was constitutionally permissible, because unlike the earlier blanket primary, it officially disregards party affiliation while allowing candidates to state their party preference. However, the court wanted to wait for more evidence before addressing the chief items in the complaint and remanded the decision to the lower courts. The link is available at: http://www.scotusblog.com/wp-content/uploads/2008/03/06-713.pdf

57   Washington State Top 2 Open Primary Facts Pave the Way for Florida, by Florida Independent Voting.Org,, available at:

http://ivn.us/2013/06/17/washington-state-top-2-open-primary-facts-pave-the-way-for-florida-2/

58   Ibid.

59   Fair Vote. When Electing More Than One Candidate in a Multi-Winner Election, available at http://www.fairvote.org/rcv -how_rcv_works

60   Ibid.

61   Fair Vote, Why IRV? at: http://archive.fairvote.org/index.php?page=1920

62   Ibid.

63   Ibid.

64   Plurality/Majority Systems at: https://www.mtholyoke.edu/acad/polit/damy/BeginnningReading/plurality.htm

65   Wikipedia, "Commission on Presidential Debates", available at https://en.wikipedia.org/wiki/Commission_on_Presidential_Debates

66   Global Strategy Group 5736. Fund for the Republic Survey 2013.12. Note: Contact author for a copy of this poll at rick@rickhubbard.org

67   Wikipedia, Chad at: https://en.wikipedia.org/wiki/Chad_(paper)

68   Wikipedia, Voter suppression in the United States, at: https://en.wikipedia.org/wiki/Voter_suppression_in_the_United_States

69   Rootstrikers at: http://www.rootstrikers.org/#!/

70   As formerly stated on the original website of: Rootstrikers, About Us, before being incorporated as a project of Demand Progress which altered the original wording.

71   Ibid.

About the Author

Rick Hubbard is a native Vermonter, retired attorney and former economic consultant, now living in South Burlington where he writes and is an activist for reforming our democracy to better serve all citizens.

Rick has a BA degree from the University of Vermont, an MBA degree from Dartmouth's Amos Tuck School of Business, and a JD degree from Georgetown University Law School.

He's a long time advocate for democracy reform who in the 1970s helped co-organize Common Cause/Vermont and subsequently, in the early 1980s, was twice elected to the national governing board of Common Cause.

In 1999 and 2000 Rick, inspired by 89-year-old "Granny D's" 18-month walk across the entire United States to highlight the need for campaign finance reform, walked with her for a week in Kentucky. Subsequently Rick walked some 450 miles around three sides of Vermont to similarly advocate through interviews with more than 50 radio, newspaper and television discussions and stories as they covered his journey.

He subsequently qualified across all party lines to raise these and other issues in the 2000 U.S. Senate race against Jim Jeffords.

More recently he has joined other activists to support of efforts by Lawrence Lessig and The New Hampshire Rebellion to encourage New Hampshire voters to ask 2016 Presidential primary candidates the question: "What specific reforms will you advance to end the corrupting influence of big money in politics?" As part of these efforts Rick has:

- Walked the length of New Hampshire, 185 miles, in January of 2014 with other NHR supporters in memory of "Granny D's" walk across the USA in 1999/2000 for Democracy Reform.

- Walked New Hampshire again in January of 2015, 150 miles, from Dixville Notch to Concord (New Hampshire's capitol) as part of 4 marches from different corners of New Hampshire to all meet at the Concord state Capital in support of Democracy Reform.

Rick walked in support of Democracy Spring's massive 140-mile march from Philadelphia's Liberty Bell to our Capitol in Washington D.C. from April 2–15, 2016 to demand that Congress take immediate action to end the corruption of big money in politics and ensure free and fair elections in which every American has an equal voice.

Once there, he was one of over 1,200 citizens peacefully arrested on the steps of the U.S. Capitol in protest that our federal political system no longer properly represents its citizens.

CPSIA information can be obtained
at www.ICGtesting.com
Printed in the USA
BVOW08s2040211216
471449BV00001B/2/P